D1622735

COCKTAILS
in NEW YORK

COCKTAILS in NEW YORK

Where to Find 100 Classics and How to Mix Them at Home

ANTHONY GIGLIO

PRINCIPAL PHOTOGRAPHY BY PETER MEDILEK

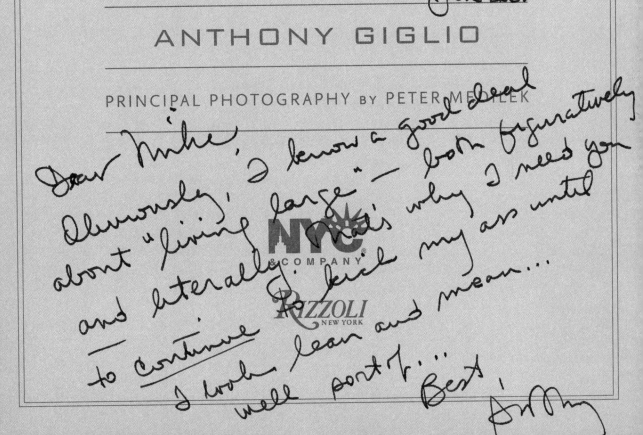

Jan 2005

Dear Mike,

Obviously, I know a good deal about "living large" — both figuratively and literally. That's why I need you to continue to kick my ass until I look lean and mean... well sort of...

Best,

RIZZOLI
NEW YORK

NYC & COMPANY

CONTENTS

PREFACE: A TOAST TO NEW YORK

JONATHAN M. TISCH & CRISTYNE L. NICHOLAS, NYC & COMPANY

*T*HE HIGHLY SUCCESSFUL *New York Restaurant Cookbook: Recipes from the Dining Capital of the World* brought great meals to your table at home. But a great meal deserves a great cocktail to start. So NYC & Company would like to invite you to enjoy some very special *Cocktails in New York*.

With its recipes for 100 classic and contemporary libations, as well as anecdotes that take you behind the scenes at some of the world's most famous establishments, *Cocktails in New York: Where to Find 100 Classics and How to Mix Them at Home* is the ultimate guide for both the cocktail connoisseur looking for new adventures, as well as the home mixologist aspiring to new heights.

Even at the height of Prohibition there were at least 30,000 watering holes operating throughout New York City. And today, visitors and New Yorkers can choose from nearly unlimited options, from the trendy to the timeless. There are glitzy velvet-roped venues with celebrity bar-keeps and hidden haunts where friends have been meeting for a quiet drink for centuries. In the eighteenth century, New Yorkers even plotted the American Revolution over a pint of ale. But cock-tails are most definitely the choice of today, with bars and restaurants creating original and inven-tive drinks that are the best in the world.

With so many exceptional bars, it can be difficult to navigate the liquid landscape. This book is designed to serve as a guide for New Yorkers and visitors alike. And while no one can truly hope to replicate the dynamic energy of New York City in their own living room, the delightful con-coctions contained herein will at least offer a small sip.

And in New York, it's always easy to enjoy cocktails responsibly since we have North Amer-ica's largest public transportation network. We encourage you to take advantage of it to arrive safely at your home or hotel.

In purchasing this book, you have also generously supported the NYC & Company Foun-dation, a charitable and educational organization whose mission is to promote New York City by supporting the arts and cultural organizations that make visiting New York a special and exciting experience. Thanks for joining us in a toast to New York City. Cheers!

FOREWORD: THE ANATOMY OF THE COCKTAIL

TONY ABOU-GANIM

*A*S A PROFESSIONAL BARTENDER, I'm often asked what I consider to be most important when mixing a cocktail. My answer is simple: Less is always more. I say this because the majority of classics that have survived the test of time are sublimely simple concoctions that adhere to this rather modest maxim. Think about it: Most classic cocktails consist of three, maybe four, ingredients at most. Take the classic dry Martini for example. It's the quintessential cocktail—the one to which all others aspire—and it consists of just two ingredients, gin and vermouth. But what separates a great Martini from less noble mixed drinks is the selection of the ingredients used in making it and how those ingredients are handled.

Craftsmanship is also important in making a cocktail, but you don't have to be a professional. With a little practice, and sound recipes, anyone can make a great cocktail. My approach to mixing drinks is both straightforward and logical, and that's what I tell customers who think they can't re-create my cocktails at home. All it takes is an understanding of the hierarchy of cocktail ingredients.

A cocktail should, first and foremost, focus on the base spirit. The base spirit—be it gin, vodka, tequila, rum, or brandy—should make up the majority of your cocktail. I often draw a comparison between cocktails and cooking: You don't grill a rib-eye steak for the béarnaise sauce, right? The sauce is important, but it's a complement to the main ingredient. Therefore, a Margarita, for example, should always be about the tequila, with the other ingredients—Cointreau and fresh lime juice—there to enhance and showcase it, not cover it up. Remember, the base spirit should define the cocktail. The Martini is a gin cocktail, and we should always taste and identify the gin with the dry vermouth acting only to enhance the enjoyment of the gin.

Now that we understand the importance of the base spirit, the remaining components of a cocktail consist of the modifiers and the accents, which we in the business call flavoring agents. These are the salt and pepper of the cocktail-making world. Modifiers include a broad range of ingredients, from aromatic wines (vermouth), to bitters (orange, Angostura, and Peychaud's), to fresh fruit juices (orange, lemon, and lime), to sugar, cream, and eggs. Accents include a plethora of liqueurs, such as Cointreau, Maraschino, and crème de cassis, as well as nonalcoholic syrups such as Rose's lime juice, orgeat, grenadine, and falernum.

When the base spirit, modifier, and accent come together in perfect balance, that is a cocktail—something far greater than the sum of its parts. And just as great chefs are constantly tasting, searching for balance and refreshment in their creations, so must the bartender. My mother was a great cook who loved to entertain, and she taught me, "Never trust a skinny chef," which isn't to say you can't trust a sober bartender, but that bartenders, like chefs, need to evaluate their own creations. Ultimately, you will be the judge of your own cocktail creations. Look for the balance of sweetness and acidity, tartness and bitterness. Consider each cocktail with all your senses and you'll create drinks that not only smell and taste great but also appeal to the eye.

So now that you understand the basic approach to making a proper, great cocktail, let the fun begin as we prepare to "mix it up!"

INTRODUCTION: HOW TO DRINK

ANTHONY GIGLIO

THE FACT THAT I'VE BEEN ABLE TO MAKE A CAREER out of writing about my favorite interests—drinking and eating—makes me something of an oddity among my family and friends and the source of endless jokes ("Thurston Howell," "Robin Leach," "The Galloping Gourmet," et al.). I suspect I'm looked upon as something of a cad or a dandy, a scammer who duped editors into thinking that I know what I'm talking about, that it's all really fun and games. To be honest, the genesis of this career path was borne out of complete boredom. In what seems like another lifetime ago I took a detour from writing about finance to learn the language of wine and spirits.

I enrolled in a wine captain's course with the Sommelier Society of America and studied under the brilliant tutelage of Master Sommelier Roger Dagorn, who shepherded me through weekly tests to earn a diploma in service that formed the foundation of my wine knowledge. From there I went to work for free at Windows on the World, where I learned how to hone my sense of taste from Kevin Zraly, who remains my idol among educators. Once I figured out how to talk about what I tasted, I set out to write about all things liquid. Along the way I earned the title Mr. Fancy Pants from those closest to me, who couldn't believe I had pulled off the transition from techie geek to drinks savant. (Maybe this book will put you on a similar path to transformation.)

Now if you imagine this kind of expertise in a young single man set loose in the streets of New York—you have a dangerous thing. My carefree barhopping evolved into an obsession with chronicling cocktails and venues to the point that I started keeping files on bars worth remembering. In my quest for knowledge, I interviewed bartenders at just about every bar I visited, discerning their techniques and researching ingredients of every shape and size. Eventually, I became a virtual reference prone to getting calls from venue-seeking friends just about every night of the week. That's when I decided it was time to commit all of this to paper in proper form: a compendium of the best recipes I could find, in bars that made drinks with attention to tradition, detail, and creativity. Thus was born Cocktails in New York. This is by no means a complete list of every great bar in Manhattan. Of the thousands that exist, this book celebrates those in which I found bartenders who, well, gave a damn about the drinks they were making.

My greatest talent, however, still lies in tasting, and thoroughly enjoying, drinks made by others. When I mix, I generally stick to the classics, or utilize a recipe that I've discovered and enjoyed, like those contained in this book. I leave the creativity to the masters like Jerry Thomas, the author of so many classics, who mixed flaming drinks and punches for New Yorkers before the turn of the century. Or his twentieth-century incarnation and my friend, Dale DeGroff, to whom almost every bartender in this book owes gratitude for reviving their profession. I've been behind the bar plenty of nights myself, and I know what a tough job it is.

Which is why I've tried to showcase recipes here that are both dynamic but, for the most part, user-friendly. I guarantee that you can make every single one of them at home, provided you remember that the spirit of making any recipe is that there's room for creative license when you don't have every single ingredient. Granted, there are a few with ingredients that are "out there"—but they're irresistibly interesting nonetheless.

And speaking of ingredients, I think that the most profound discovery I made while writing this book was the lengths to which many of this book's bartenders go to be innovative when creating a new drink or putting a twist on something old. New York bartenders are always on the cutting edge, and that's why cocktail crazes always begin here. (It's also part of why a book documenting this city's creativity is worthwhile.) From cactus-pear purees to lychee nuts, rose petals to homemade brandied cherries, these recipes show a flair for creativity and ingenuity that would leave many chain-restaurant bartenders scratching their heads. That's because we're at a moment in time, cocktail-wise, when we're still rediscovering the dynamism that inspired our pre-Prohibition forefathers, who two centuries ago began mixing spirits with tinctures and fruit juices, first modestly, then eventually with great style, to create cocktails of distinction. If Jerry Thomas were here today, I imagine he'd be impressed with the state of cocktails at the venues listed in this book—well, after he got over the shock of seeing women on both sides of the bar.

I dare say, however, that Thomas might not recognize many of the drinks listed in this book beyond the first chapter, "Proven Classics." Indeed, the subsequent seven chapters celebrate the nonstandards, from the "New Standards" to "Mixologist Mixed," from "Creative License" to "Secret Ingredients." And for those hard-to-find ingredients there's a Sources section on page 233 that'll help. Scattered throughout the book you'll find tips and trivia that lend insight into each recipe; you'll also be able to cross-reference your favorite liquors and flavors in the back (see page 246). Lastly, there are icons accompanying each recipe that indicate the type of glass in which to serve the drink. The chart on page 13 explains their exact sizes. Of course, you should feel free to improvise with whatever you have at hand, though I beg you to eschew plastic tumblers at all costs. All recipes are intended to yield one serving, unless otherwise noted.

If one point unifies most of the recipes, it's that the cocktails should be served in a chilled glass. All that means is that you should put ice and water in the glass while you're mixing the other ingredients according to the directions. Then, just before you strain the drink into the glass, you should dump out the water and ice. Now the glass is chilled and ready to keep the drink cold. Among the basic components you'll need to have on hand for many drinks (see page 11), there are a couple that you should make from scratch: For simple syrup, combine equal amounts of sugar and water in a small saucepan and bring to a boil while stirring. Reduce heat and continue stirring until sugar dissolves. Let cool and transfer to a clean, airtight jar. This keeps in the refrigerator indefinitely. Another staple, sour mix, can be made by first preparing simple syrup. Then while it's still hot, add one equal part each lemon and lime juice. Stir until dissolved. This keeps for several months in the refrigerator. Another technique mentioned frequently is "topping," which simply means what it sounds like. If the recipe calls for a topping of Champagne, then prepare the drink, reserving enough room at the top of the glass for a splash of bubbly, or whatever is called for. With a little practice this all comes quite naturally.

And that's the point of this book, to take inspiration from the bartenders who've inspired me to make cocktails properly, but not stoically. If anything, I've tried to impart the sense of dynamism that went into creating—or re-creating—these drinks, and hope that it makes you want to take the book to the kitchen and start shaking up cocktails. And again, if you don't have every single ingredient at hand, follow the lead of so many great bartenders in this great city of ours and use your imagination.

STOCKING THE HOME BAR

SAVORY INGREDIENTS
Tomato Juice
Clam Juice
Horseradish
Hot Sauces
Worcestershire Sauce

SWEETENING INGREDIENTS
Simple Syrup
Sour Mix
Powdered Sugar
Granulated Sugar
Coconut Cream
Various Fruit Syrups
(Orgeat, Elderflower)
Grenadine

BITTERS
Angostura Bitters
Peychaud's Bitters
Orange Bitters

SODAS
Seltzer/Club Soda
Quinine/Tonic Water
Various: Cola, Lemon/Lime, etc.

FRUIT JUICES
Lime Juice
Lemon Juice
Cranberry Juice
Pineapple Juice
Other juices and nectars

DAIRY/EGG INGREDIENTS
Milk
Cream (Heavy, Half & Half)
Butter
Eggs

GARNISHES
Lemon Wedges
Lime Wedges
Assorted Fruit Wheels
Pineapple Chunks
Maraschino Cherries
Olives
Celery
Fresh Herbs (Mint, Basil, etc.)

TOOLS FOR THE HOME BAR

BOSTON SHAKER: Two-piece set comprised of a mixing glass and a slightly larger metal container that acts as a cover for the mixing glass for shaking cocktails. The mixing glass can be used alone for stirring drinks that aren't shaken.

BARSPOON: A long-handled shallow spoon with a twisted handle used for stirring drinks.

HAWTHORNE STRAINER: A perforated metal top for the metal half of a Boston shaker, held in place by a wire coil, that serves as a strainer.

JULEP STRAINER: A perforated, spoon-shaped strainer used in conjunction with a mixing glass.

COCKTAIL SHAKER: A metal pitcher with a tight-fitting lid, under which sits a strainer. While styles vary widely, popular retro-style pitchers have a handle as well as a spout that's sealed with a twist-off cap.

ELECTRIC BLENDER: Absolutely necessary to make frozen drinks, puree fruit, and crush ice for certain recipes.

CUTTING BOARD: Either wood or plastic board used to cut up fruit for garnishes.

PARING KNIFE: Small, sharp knife to prepare fruit for garnishes.

MUDDLER: Looks like a wooden pestle, the flat end of which is used to crush and combine ingredients in a serving glass or mixing glass.

GRATER: Useful for zesting fruit or grating nutmeg.

BOTTLE OPENER: Essential for opening bottles that don't have twist-off caps.

CHURCH KEY: Usually metal, the key is pointed at one end to punch holes in the tops of cans, while the other end is used to open bottles.

CORKSCREW: There are myriad styles from which to choose; professionals use the "Waiter's Corkscrew," which looks like a penknife, the "Screw-Pull," or "Rabbit" corkscrews. The "Winged Corkscrew," found in most homes, is considered easiest to use but often destroys the cork.

CITRUS REAMER: Essential for juicing fruit; comes in two styles, either the strainer bowl with the pointed cone on top, or the wooden handle with the cone attached, which must be used with a strainer.

JIGGER: Helpful for precise measuring (though pros just count out the ounces in seconds silently), the jigger is usually two V-shaped metal cups conjoined at the narrow end, one end measuring 1 ounce, the other 1½ ounces.

ICE BUCKET WITH SCOOP AND TONGS: A bar without ice is like a car without gas. Use the scoop—never the glass—to gather ice in a mixing glass or shaker, and tongs to add single cubes to a prepared drink.

MISCELLANEOUS ACCOUTREMENTS: Sip sticks or stirrers, straws, cocktail napkins, coasters, cocktail picks.

GLASSWARE FOR THE HOME BAR

COCKTAIL GLASS (alias **MARTINI GLASS**): Typically 4–8 ounces, but lately much larger

HURRICANE GLASS
Short stem, hourglass-shaped, typically 14–20 ounces

BRANDY SNIFTER
A squat, teardrop-shaped glass, typically 6 ounces

COLLINS GLASS
Tall and narrow, typically 8–12 ounces

ROCKS GLASS
Wide and squat, typically 8 ounces

MARGARITA GLASS
A curvier cocktail glass, about 12 ounces

HIGHBALL GLASS
Shorter Collins glass, typically 8–10 ounces

WINE GLASS
Standard is 8–12 ounces; other shapes exist for certain wines

CHAMPAGNE FLUTE
A tall, stemmed glass with a small mouth, typically 6 ounces

Chapter 1

PROVEN CLASSICS

CLASSIC MARTINI

THE RED SNAPPER

MESA GRILL MARGARITA

THE BELLINI

MANHATTAN

SIDECAR

WHISKEY SOUR

RUSTY NAIL

BLOODY MARY

PROHIBITION PUNCH

OLD TOWN OLD-FASHIONED

BRONX COCKTAIL

CLASSIC MARTINI

THE FOUR SEASONS

I DARESAY IT WOULD BE DOWNRIGHT INAPPROPRIATE to drink any other cocktail here than a Classic Martini, made in its original form with gin instead of vodka. After all, that's what many of the power brokers drank as they lunched here when the Four Seasons opened in 1959—when vodka's popularity was in ascension but not quite there yet. Fittingly—if not miraculously—the bar still looks exactly as it did back then, thanks to the restaurant's status as the only Manhattan restaurant interior designated as an architectural landmark, a testament to its designers, Mies van der Rohe and Philip Johnson. Although this restaurant is known for power meals among movers and shakers, the bar is where it all begins, in the clubby Grill Room, with its rosewood walls, soaring ceiling, leather banquettes, and rippling brass curtains. A septuagenarian barman who's been here since the beginning would be all too perfect, but the mixed bag of expert tenders here get it right—even if they pour vodka for their own Martinis.

The Four Seasons' Classic Martini calls for the gin to be stirred gently, which means in a swift, fluid manner. This is best achieved with a barspoon, which is a spoon with a long, thin handle. What makes it different than a regular spoon is that, because of its sleekness, it moves gracefully amid the ice cubes.

½ ounce dry vermouth

3½ ounces Tanqueray No. Ten

3 small green olives

1 Into an ice-filled cocktail shaker, pour dry vermouth; swirl liquid around in shaker.

2 Toss out both ice and vermouth.

3 Add new ice and the gin, and then stir gently until chilled.

4 Strain into a chilled **COCKTAIL GLASS.** Garnish with 3 small olives.

THE RED SNAPPER

KING COLE BAR AND LOUNGE

HE St. Regis is considered one of the very best hotels in the city and as such is expected to have one hell of a great cocktail bar. It does. The King Cole Bar is legendary for a number of reasons, the most important of which for cocktail lovers is the perfecting of the Red Snapper—otherwise known as the Bloody Mary. The bar itself is a magnificent little rectangle of a room with towering ceilings, brocade banquettes, and the famous Maxfield Parrish mural of Old King Cole looming large over the din. The service is anachronistic, with bartenders paying pre-Prohibition attention to details (meaning that nobody is squeezing lemons into your drink with questionably clean bare hands), and attendants keep the room impeccably neat despite the traffic. Speaking of which, consider that the business set typically book tables ahead, so if you want to guarantee a seat, do the same. You won't be disappointed.

A general rule of thumb among many bartenders, as among chefs, is that a recipe is a guide, rather than a rule. This philosophy couldn't be more appropriate for The Red Snapper because the level of spiciness is absolutely subjective. If you're making it at home, feel free to play with the quantities of peppers and Worcestershire sauce to find the balance that's right for you.

2 pinches of salt

2 pinches of black pepper

2 pinches of cayenne pepper

3 dashes of Worcestershire sauce

1 dash of fresh lemon juice

1½ ounces vodka

2 ounces tomato juice

1 lemon wheel

1 In a cocktail shaker, combine salt, pepper, cayenne, Worcestershire sauce, and lemon juice.

2 Add ice, vodka, and tomato juice.

3 Cover and shake thoroughly.

4 Strain into an ice-filled HIGHBALL GLASS. Garnish with the lemon wheel.

Few cocktail recipes are as laden with lore as the Bloody Mary. I often joke that if the spicy concoction were a real person, Mary's story would make for a compelling soap opera. Conceived by accident in Paris in the 1920s, when her father Fernand Petiot, a barman at Harry's New York Bar, unwittingly mixes vodka with tomato juice and gives birth to a cocktail he is unable—or unwilling—to name. Enter Roy Barton, an entertainer who witnesses the birth and says that the bracing redhead reminds him of a Mary he once knew at a Chicago club called the Bucket of Blood—et voilà: The Bloody Mary is christened. Fast forward a decade to 1934, and Petiot becomes a bartender at the St. Regis in New York. He readies Bloody Mary for her society debut by dressing her up with salt, pepper, and lemon juice, and splashes her with Worcestershire sauce for perfume. Her name, however, is immediately scorned as offensive in this most haute of hotels, and she is forced to assume a new identity: Red Snapper. Secretly, however, even the snobs prefer her real name and Mary reclaims her birthright and prevails as the toast of the King Cole Bar. Her reputation precedes her wherever she goes and she becomes an international phenomenon. Later in life she is immortalized as the patron saint of brunches and hangovers. Back at the St. Regis, they officially prefer to call her Red Snapper, but you can call her what you like.

MESA GRILL MARGARITA

WHILE CHEF BOBBY FLAY GETS DUE PROPS for his innovative American Southwestern fare at this spacious, colorful restaurant, behind the scenes is co-owner Lawrence Kretchmer, a man so passionate about tequila that he wrote a book about it a few years back. Kretchmer is of the mindset that many of his forty or so varieties of carefully chosen, high-end tequilas don't need to be mixed into cocktails at all. I'd have to agree, but it would be a shame to miss the Mesa Grill Prickly Pear Margarita, made with cactus pear juice, or the straightforward Mesa Grill Margarita, which I believe is one of the very best in the city. Then go on and order one of Flay's Shrimp and Roasted Garlic Corn Tamales and pair it with a Corralejo Reposado, an exceptionally smooth tequila that tastes fantastic on its own, but would also—to Kretchmer's chagrin—make a memorable contribution to a well-made Margarita.

Triple sec is one of those mysterious liqueurs that promotes healthy debates among cocktail aficionados. Generic triple sec is a clear, potent, orange-flavored liqueur that, despite its name (which translates as "triple dry") is actually somewhat sweet—although not necessarily cloying. In addition to the generic stuff, there are curaçao (the orange, not the blue, is the more traditional), and upscale, brand-name versions, such as Cointreau and Grand Marnier. In Margaritas, the latter two are often used as "upgrades."

2 ounces white tequila

1 ounce triple sec or other orange liqueur

2 ounces fresh lime juice

1 lime twist

Coarse salt (optional)

1 In a cocktail shaker, combine tequila, triple sec, and lime juice.

2 Add ice, cover, and shake vigorously.

3 Strain into an ice-filled **COLLINS GLASS.** Garnish with the lime twist. If you prefer, before pouring rub a lime wedge around the glass rim and dip the glass into a saucer of coarse salt.

THE BELLINI

FEW PUBLIC VENUES IN THE CITY OFFER VIEWS AS SPECTACULAR as those at Rainbow Grill, the bar adjacent to the famous Rainbow Room, up on the sixty-fifth floor of 30 Rockefeller Plaza. The first time I had a cocktail here I found bartending legend Dale "King Cocktail" DeGroff behind the bar, the Empire State Building and Downtown lights twinkling around him, making drinks with great fanfare and aplomb. Today the Rainbow Grill is a restaurant and piano bar run by the Cipriani family, that famous Venetian famiglia that owns Harry's Bars and eponymous restaurants worldwide. Their signature drink here is their signature just about everywhere: the Bellini, an often-imitated but seldom correctly made mixture of sweet, mouthwatering white peaches and ice-cold prosecco. Arrigo Cipriani, who wrote The Harry's Bar Cookbook, says that there was a time when the Bellini was seasonal, only available from June through September. "Now we are lucky—we can get excellent frozen white peach puree from France and serve Bellinis year-round."

2 ounces white peach puree

6 ounces prosecco

1 Into a chilled **CHAMPAGNE FLUTE** pour peach puree.

2 Top with prosecco up to the rim.

To make the best Bellini possible, Arrigo Cipriani, author of The Harry's Bar Cookbook, says: "Never use yellow peaches to make a Bellini and never puree the peaches by machine. If you can't find the frozen puree, you'll just have to produce it the old-fashioned way—using a food mill or meat grinder to make the pulp and then forcing it through a fine sieve. If the peach puree is very tart, sweeten it with just a little sugar syrup. Most importantly, the peach puree and the prosecco should be ice-cold."

Arrigo Cipriani's Bellini calls for prosecco, an Italian style of sparkling wine that's usually of very good quality and reasonably priced. It's made primarily in the district of Valdobbiadene, in the region of Veneto—where Venice is located. Prosecco is also the name of the grape used to make this sparkling wine, which at its best produces delicate, stone-fruit flavors and aromatics. The reason it's so affordable—when compared with Champagne, for example—is that it's not made in the costly methode champenoise, or classic method, but rather the Charmat method of sparkling wine, which is far less expensive, yielding a fresh, young wine best consumed within a year of production. Producers to look for include Bisol, Martini & Rossi, Mionetto, and Nino Franco.

MANHATTAN

*L*ONG BEFORE THE (THANKFULLY WANING) ERA of the theme restaurant—by some seventy years—there was Monkey Bar, replete with famous murals of forty-six frolicking monkeys painted by a variety of artists, monkey light fixtures, and monkey designs just about everywhere, even on the carpeting. Back in the 1930s, this beautiful supper club–style lounge in the Hotel Elysée hosted the swank set who came for risqué entertainment, dimly lit canoodling, and dinner in the elegant dining room behind the bar. These days, after a pricey renovation, the dark-wooded bar is packed with expense account types and their arm candy. What better place than under the gaze of so many looming primates to sip the classic drink named after this great jungle island.

Most spirits producers strive for unwavering consistency—the liquor is tested and blended so that it tastes the same from bottle to bottle and from year to year. Taking a cue from the wine world, Jack Daniel's has departed from this philosophy with its Single Barrel line. Each bottle can taste different—for example showing more oak or more caramel. But no matter what bottling, you're sure to get a rich, smooth, and not-to-sweet whiskey.

2 ounces Jack Daniel's Single Barrel Whiskey

1 ounce sweet vermouth

2 dashes Angostura bitters

1 maraschino cherry

1 In a cocktail shaker, combine the whiskey, vermouth, and bitters.

2 Add ice, cover, and shake thoroughly.

3 Strain into a chilled COCKTAIL GLASS.

4 Garnish with the cherry.

SIDECAR

*A*LL IS NOT AS IT SEEMS AT THIS SLEEK, CHIC WATERING HOLE, where the legendary all-glass unisex bathrooms are talked about as much as the seriously made cocktails. In fact, the cocktail menu is far more serious than the food menu, which one would expect to feature veggiecentric minimalist concoctions to match the décor, when in fact it features high-end burgers and fries. Each cocktail, however, is listed with place of origin, the year it was invented (which, like all bar lore, is undoubtedly subject to debate), and some background that can be expanded upon by any of the serious bartenders. My favorite here is the Sidecar: "Origin: Paris 1916. Our recipe comes from Harry's New York Bar in Paris, circa World War I." This is about the last place in town where I'd expect to find this dark, old-fashioned classic, given Bar 89's modern, skylit surroundings, but the barmen build their Sidecars as if channeling the ghosts of their speakeasy-era predecessors.

1 lemon wedge
Granulated sugar
3 ounces brandy
1½ ounces Cointreau
1½ ounces fresh lemon juice

1 Rub the rim of a chilled **COCKTAIL GLASS** with the pulpy side of the lemon wedge. Pour a few tablespoons of the sugar onto a plate. Twirl the glass rim in the sugar to coat.

2 Into an ice-filled cocktail shaker pour the remaining ingredients.

3 Cover and shake thoroughly.

4 Strain into the prepared cocktail glass.

Few bars can claim that a single classic drink originated under their roof, but Harry's New York Bar in Paris can boast at least three. Besides popularizing both the Sidecar and the Bloody Mary, Harry's was responsible for the French 75, named after a 75-millimeter field gun used in World War I. To make the drink, combine 1½ ounces of gin, 2 teaspoons of sugar, and 1½ ounces of lemon juice in an ice-filled shaker and shake. Pour into a cocktail glass, top with champagne, and garnish with an orange slice and cherry. Or, of course, you can make the trek to Paris to have it prepared at Harry's New York Bar and pay your respects to the famous bar itself.

WHISKEY SOUR

WHEN PATROON OPENED IN 1996, they were catering to dot-com consumption, a party in which I, as an online editor, giddily took part. But nearly a decade later, the midtown restaurant has snuffed the cigar bar and eased into a less ostentatious form of decadence. It's still basically a boys' club. A place where powerful midtown men come to chill with cronies in a leather banquette and chew on the day's business and one of chef John Villa's classic dishes, Duck à l'Orange, Steak Diana (which owes its name to the owner's wife), or Bananas Foster. Patroon does equal justice to that classic king of sours, the Whiskey Sour. Forget the amaretto, this is the only sour a self-respecting power broker can drink. And at Patroon, the house pour is Jack Daniel's, an exceptionally smooth and rather woody-tasting whiskey that just happens to be the perfect accompaniment to one of Villa's steaks cooked over maple and hickory embers.

Jack Daniel's may be your favorite whiskey, but it certainly is not your favorite bourbon. You see, Jack belongs to a smaller niche of American hooch called Tennessee whiskey, distinct from bourbon because it goes through a charcoal-filtering process. Taste it side-by-side with the stuff from the Bluegrass state and the distinctive flavor becomes apparent. If you're partial to the stuff, I can also recommend George Dickel, another brand of Tennessee whiskey.

1½ ounces Jack Daniel's Tennessee Whiskey
½ ounce fresh lemon juice
½ ounce fresh lime juice
1¼ ounces simple syrup
1 lemon wheel
1 maraschino cherry

1 In an ice-filled cocktail shaker, combine the whiskey, juices, and syrup.

2 Cover and shake thoroughly.

3 Strain into an ice-filled ROCKS GLASS.

4 Garnish with the lemon wheel and maraschino cherry both on a toothpick.

RUSTY NAIL

*O*N MY FIRST VISIT TO SMITH & WOLLENSKY over a decade ago, I made the mistake of asking bartender Paddy Ford what microbrews they offered. To my utter embarrassment, Paddy bellowed to the entire bar, "Whoaa, fancy pants wants a microbrew!" See, Smith & Wollensky isn't much for fads. Big slabs of dry-aged beef never seem to go out of style in this city, and even when diet docs warned against them, it never mattered to the folks here. And the same philosophy goes for Paddy's classic cocktails, like a super-dry Dirty Martini—rumor has it that the same bottle of vermouth has been here since they opened—or a Manhattan made with the traditional rye whiskey. Later that first night, determined not to be caught with my fancy pants down a second time, I followed the lead of the silver-haired gent ahead of me and ordered a Rusty Nail—a drink that earned a nod of approval from Paddy.

There's no substitute for Drambuie, a honey and herbal liqueur from Scotland, when mixing this drink. It often strikes the uninitiated as quite medicinal on the first sip, but stick with it; it may seduce you by the last.

1½ ounces Scotch
1 ounce Drambuie
1 lemon twist

1 Combine Scotch and Drambuie in a **ROCKS GLASS** with ice.

2 Stir gently.

3 Garnish with the lemon twist.

BLOODY MARY

EW BARS CAN CLAIM CENTRAL PARK AS THEIR FRONT YARD. And no others offer panoramic murals of old New York by Everett Shinn as an alternate view, but this grand old bar has both. The massive, oak-paneled room was a brokerage house until the Great Depression, when it was wisely converted to a bar. And although the room still evokes cigars and testosterone, thankfully, times do change: Now, both men sans jacket and even women are free to sit for a drink. (The latter since only 1974.) The popular bar is generally bustling and the banquettes with the park view are the most coveted seats in the house. In order to score one, I like to arrive soon after the 11:30 am opening, and jump-start the day with an Oak Bar Bloody Mary. The drink comes garnished with two golf ball–size olives and a shrimp—a touch of sustenance for the matutinal drinker that doesn't err on the side of becoming a salad.

Another of the great hidden art gems of New York, the murals in the Oak Bar were painted in the 1940s by Everett Shinn, part of a group of realist painters dubbed the Ashcan School. Shinn, who arrived in New York in 1897, painted average citizens and everyday events in the city—workers and slum residents, fires and evictions—capturing scenes that previous artists had deemed unworthy of painting.

For an especially refreshing Bloody Mary, try making your own tomato juice. Coarsely chop a few fresh tomatoes and puree them in a blender. Then strain to remove seeds, skin, and pulp.

2 ounces vodka

Splash of beef broth

Splash of Tabasco

Splash of Worcestershire sauce

½ ounce fresh lemon juice

5 ounces tomato juice

½ teaspoon prepared horseradish

1 lime wedge

2 Queen olives or other large green olives

1 shrimp, poached, peeled, and chilled

1 Combine the first seven ingredients in a large glass with several ice cubes.

2 Using another equal-size glass "roll" the drink by pouring it back and forth several times.

3 Garnish with the lime wedge, olives, and peeled shrimp.

PROHIBITION PUNCH

CAMPBELL APARTMENT

*L*OCATED IN GRAND CENTRAL TERMINAL, Campbell Apartment takes its name from John W. Campbell, the mogul who held court here beginning in the 1920s. This lavish, one-of-a-kind space once served as both his personal office and A-list-only salon. However, by the 1950s it was a forgotten time capsule, used as a signalman's office and a jail. In a Sistine Chapel–like renovation, the stone fireplace, leaded glass windows, and elaborate painted ceiling have been returned to their original glory for the enjoyment of commuters and would-be robber barons. There's even a floor safe, a relic from the pre-Visa era. The cocktails, too, take their inspiration from the Prohibition years. Period drinks like the Bayard Fizz clink glasses with house originals like the Prohibition Punch. "The Prohibition Punch, which is our biggest seller, borrows from the ingredients of the drinks of the '20s. It's our creation, but everything here remains rooted in the classics," says owner Mark Grossich.

1 ounce Appleton Estate Rum V/X
½ ounce Grand Marnier
2 ounces passion fruit juice
Splash of cranberry juice
Splash of fresh lemon juice
1 ounce Moët et Chandon Champagne

1 Combine the rum, Grand Marnier, and fruit juices with ice in a **BRANDY SNIFTER**, and stir gently.

2 Top with the Champagne.

Appleton Estate Rum is a Jamaican dark rum that also works well in the classic Planter's Punch, in which 1 ounce of dark rum, ½ ounce orgeat syrup, 2 ounces of orange juice, and one ounce of pineapple juice are shaken together in an ice-filled shaker. Served in an ice-filled snifter or Collins glass, the punch is garnished with a lime wedge or maraschino cherry.

The Beaux Arts Grand Central Terminal, completed in 1913, has reclaimed its status as a city within the city. From the fine marketplace offering the freshest fish, cheeses, and produce, to the food court and decadent retail shopping, this soaring public space is far more than a commuter hub.

OLD TOWN OLD-FASHIONED

OLD TOWN BAR & GRILL

)))HETHER YOU'RE TALKING WHISKEY, family recipes, or taverns, everyone claims to be "olde." But having been established in 1892, this Union Square joint truly is. And if there's a lesson to be learned from Old Town, it's that the secret to bar longevity must be a good burger and a strong Old-Fashioned. Old Town wears its age well, with two stories of dark wood booths and a pressed tin ceiling. It offers the kind of warm, well-worn atmosphere that's a genuine comfort on those days when life kicks your ass. And judging by the 5:00 pm crowd, lots of people share the sentiment. Sure, signature drinks and velvet ropes are a guaranteed write-up in the Sunday Styles section, but a year later, the bar's a footnote and you're reminiscing about it over brews—or this perfect Old Fashioned—at the Old Town.

Many bartenders will muddle an additional orange slice and cherry with the initial sugar and bitters. That makes for a fruitier, sweeter drink, but personally I like the Old Town's no-nonsense approach.

½ teaspoon sugar
6 drops bitters
1½ ounces Virginia Gentleman Bourbon
Splash of soda
Maraschino cherry
Half-moon slice of orange

1 Combine the sugar and bitters in a ROCKS GLASS and soften with a spoon or muddler.

2 Add ice, followed by the bourbon and splash of soda.

3 Stir gently.

4 Garnish with the cherry and orange slice.

BRONX COCKTAIL

BULL AND BEAR

*A*TTEMPTING TO PICK A SINGLE COCKTAIL to characterize this legendary bar, located on the ground floor of the Waldorf-Astoria, is as daunting as picking a winning stock off the room's electronic ticker—although in reality, far less risky. Among the blue-chip cocktails that got their start here are the Bobbie Burns, the Rob Roy, and, most notably, the Bronx. Although less familiar than its interborough sibling, the Manhattan, the Bronx ranks among the cocktail greats. According to his memoirs, barman Johnnie Solon was challenged by a lunch customer to create a new drink. His answer: the Bronx, which became an instant hit. Having just a few days prior visited New York's famous Bronx Zoo, Solon named the drink in its honor, noting, "Customers used to tell me of the strange animals they saw after a lot of mixed drinks." The bull and bear poised over the bar, however, are century-old sentinels cast in bronze, so don't blame them on The Bronx.

The Bull and Bear pays tribute to the Men's Bar, located in the original Waldorf, now the site of the Empire State Building. Certainly politically incorrect by today's standards, the name Men's Bar evidently wasn't much more popular a hundred years ago. In fact, everyone took to calling the place the Bull and Bear for the bronzes that decorated it. Now the statues reside here and the name is finally official.

3 ounces gin
1½ ounces fresh orange juice
Dash of French dry vermouth
Dash of Italian sweet vermouth
1 orange twist

1 In an ice-filled cocktail shaker, combine all liquid ingredients.

2 Cover and shake thoroughly.

3 Strain into a chilled **COCKTAIL GLASS.**

4 Garnish with orange twist.

To make an orange twist sure to impress, use a special tool called a channel kinife and start peeling from the top of the fruit going downwards in a spiral form.

Chapter 2

NEW STANDARDS

CLASSIC MOJITO

RUM JULEP

SPANISH MANHATTAN

GREENWICH FIZZ

BLOODY CLAM

SUMMER SANGRIA

POMEGRANATE MARTINI

RED CAT DARK 'N STORMY

PEAR MARTINI

PISCO SOUR

THE BIGGER APPLE MARTINI

PARADISE MARTINI

CAIPIRINHA

NEW YORK SOUR

LYCHEE BELLINI

CLASSIC MOJITO

*M*OJITOS, THOSE MOUTHWATERING, RUMMY LIME-AND-MINT-INFUSED COCKTAILS from Cuba, are up there with Cosmos, Margaritas, and Manhattans among New Yorkers' favorite cocktails. Few concoctions, however, fit their surroundings as thoroughly as the beautiful, mint-garnished Mojitos made at Calle Ocho. Named for the street running through Miami's Little Havana district, this Upper West Side bar throbs with equatorial excitement: boldly colorful décor, loud, seductive Latino music, and a crowd that moves to *la musica* with drinks in hand. Such energy could have everything to do with the high sugar level—via simple syrup—in this potent elixir, which is deceptively balanced by fresh lime juice. Just like Caipirinhas—also made expertly here—Mojitos go down like lemonade, and don't register on the hangover Richter scale until the next morning. Thankfully, at that point, Happy Hour is only eight hours away.

Fresh mint is essential to this drink—in fact, without it you can't make a Mojito. The sugar cane skewer, however, isn't essential, but a flourish meant to impress. Look for sugar cane, chopped up, at a Caribbean specialty market or a Latin bodega. Peel and cut them into lengths taller than the glass you're using.

8 to 10 mint leaves
2 ounces fresh lime juice
2 ounces simple syrup
2½ ounces light rum
1 whole mint sprig
1 sugar cane skewer (optional)

1 In a cocktail shaker, combine mint leaves, lime juice, and simple syrup; muddle thoroughly.

2 Add rum and top with ice.

3 Cover and shake thoroughly.

4 Strain into an ice-filled **ROCKS GLASS** (or **COLLINS GLASS**).

5 Garnish with the sprig of mint and/or a sugar cane skewer.

RUM JULEP

THE BAR AT THIS GRAND, BOISTEROUS RESTAURANT, located in an 1862 landmark cast-iron Tribeca building, is exactly what owner/chef Henry Meer would like it to be: a meeting place for locals, an elegant tavern in a cavernous restaurant, modeled on the legendary New York food halls of yesteryear. But anachronistic flourishes abound and the presence of female bartenders and high-tech flat-screen televisions keep imbibers' feet planted firmly in the twenty-first century. Still, I was surprised to find that the timeless Mint Julep —which is much older than this building—was made here with rum instead of bourbon. As I sipped one recently on a warm afternoon, it dawned on me why it fits this space so perfectly: In the entrance hall, just before the bar room, dozens of shellfish and mollusks sit on beds of ice, waiting to be served with lemon wedges and mignonette sauce. What better complement to a *plateau de fruits de mer* than a citrus-kissed, minty-fresh Julep, made with relatively light, lemon-flavored rum? Makes sense to me now.

Even though this isn't a "proper" Julep in the Kentucky Derby sense—where bourbon is mandatory—the attention to detail is no less important, specifically when it comes to the ice. Purists claim that the ice should be crushed. The crushed ice, when tightly packed, doesn't dilute the drink, but helps it to last longer and to form the trademark frost on the glass. For a classic Mint Julep, omit the lime, lime juice, and club soda, and replace the rum with bourbon.

A few mint leaves
1 lime, cut into 4 wedges
Splash of lime juice
1 teaspoon raw sugar
1½ ounces Bacardi Limón
Splash of club soda
1 lime wheel

1 In a cocktail shaker, muddle the mint, lime wedges, lime juice, and sugar.

2 Add the rum, and then ice.

3 Cover and shake thoroughly.

4 Strain into a **COLLINS GLASS** filled with crushed ice (see Tip).

5 Finish with a splash of soda. Garnish with the lime wheel.

SPANISH MANHATTAN

I DON'T THINK IT'S A COINCIDENCE that Suba sounds a lot like scuba, given how much water there is all over this tri-level Spanish hotspot. Downstairs there's a subterranean moat, which surrounds a dining island with a shimmering reflecting pool. Next door is a cavernous, skylit chamber, and upstairs is a crowded bar where in the early evening the tapas are free, and the cocktails are inspired by the throbbing Latin music. I'm a big Manhattan fan and was therefore intrigued to try the Spanish Manhattan here, which is made with bourbon—as it should be—but brilliantly employs sweet oloroso sherry in lieu of sweet vermouth. The effect is subtle, but nonetheless startling and logical in this barrio environment. My hat is off to bartender Nicholas Hernandez, who teaches a monthly "Cocktail Camp" here to teach ordinary Joes how to make 'em like pros.

Oloroso is a rich, brown, full-bodied style of sherry that's been sweetened by a concentrate called *dulce* made with Pedro Ximenez grapes. It's actually pretty easy to find at a decent retail shop, especially one specializing in Spanish wines.

2 ounces Maker's Mark

1 ounce Lustau Sherry

2 dashes Peychaud's Bitters

1 In an ice-filled cocktail shaker, combine the bourbon, sherry, and bitters.

2 Stir and strain into a chilled **COCKTAIL GLASS.**

GREENWICH FIZZ

ITH EXPOSED BRICK WALLS AND DRAMATIC LIGHTING, the Grill is one of those Downtown restaurants that feels as if it's been around for fifty years—even though it was only opened in 1990. That vibe is reinforced with a magnificent mahogany bar (one that veteran barflies may recognize from 1970s haunt Maxwell's Plum at First Avenue and 64th Street). Even some cocktails, like the Greenwich Fizz, pay homage to another era. First, this cocktail uses gin, the preferred tipple of Prohibition-era drinks. Now, I know what you're saying: I hate gin. Well guess what, most people hated it in the Roaring Twenties too, and their gin was a whole lot worse than ours, which is why cocktails became so popular. Get it? In this drink, the trick to tempering gin is a shot of Maraschino, a delicious, clear Italian liqueur distilled from Marasca cherries, that has nothing at all to do with those red sundae toppers.

The fizz is a classic type of drink that uses soda water to add bubbles to the mix. A Sloe Gin Fizz, perhaps the best-known example of this category, uses sloe gin, made from a type of wild plum called the blackthorn. Sloe gin isn't really a true "gin" at all; while it has a gin base, it has a very sweet flavor rather than gin's distinctive dry taste. To make a Sloe Gin Fizz, combine 1½ ounces of sloe gin with 3 ounces of lemon juice in an ice-filled shaker, shake, and strain into an ice-filled highball glass. Top off with soda and garnish with a cherry.

Just above the Tribeca Grill is the Tribeca Film Center—both are housed in a landmark building—making the Grill a favorite haunt of stars and cinephiles alike. The restaurant has hosted parties for the likes of Nelson Mandela and Bruce Springsteen. The upstairs screening room holds movie premieres in addition to the annual film festival.

2 ounces gin
1 ounce Maraschino liqueur
½ ounce fresh lime juice
3 ounces ginger ale
1 piece candied ginger, about 2 inches long

1 In an ice-filled cocktail shaker, combine the gin, liqueur, and lime juice.

2 Cover and shake thoroughly.

3 Strain into a **HIGHBALL GLASS** filled with ice.

4 Top with ginger ale. Garnish with the piece of candied ginger.

BLOODY CLAM

GRAND CENTRAL OYSTER BAR

I'VE ALWAYS THOUGHT THAT THE NAME of this legendary restaurant is somehow falsely modest. After all, an oyster bar would imply simply that: a bar, piled with oysters atop crushed ice, around which people sit. But this magnificent space, which looks much as it did when it opened more than ninety years ago, is really several venues under one beautifully designed Rafael Guastavino tile roof. In addition to the actual oyster bar, there's the Saloon, the main dining room, and the white-vinyl lounge area. My favorite spot is the oyster bar proper, where more than 30 varieties of impeccably fresh oysters are available. Though a crisp, dry Sancerre from the excellent wine list is a logical partner to these bivalve beauties, I like the idea of balancing the cool, briny oysters with a little heat by way of the Bloody Clam. The name, of course, may not be the most enticing in history, but neither is that of its inspiration, the Bloody Mary, which has done just fine. Be warned that the Bloody Clam sets the spice and heat bars higher than the modest Mary.

If you can't find wasabi powder, you could easily substitute the dry mustard that's available in every supermarket's spice section. As for the Sriracha sauce, it's a spicy, clear-your-sinuses chili sauce that really has no match, but if you can't find it at an Asian grocery, you could substitute Tabasco or any other chili sauce.

1 shucked littleneck clam
1½ ounces premium vodka
4 ounces Clamato Tomato Cocktail
1 ounce clam juice
Pinch of wasabi powder (see Tip)
Dash of Thai Sriracha Sauce (see Tip)
Dash of Worcestershire sauce
Juice of ¼ lemon
Juice of ¼ lime

1 Into a tall **COLLINS GLASS** drop the clam and cover it with ice.

2 Into an ice-filled cocktail shaker, pour all remaining ingredients.

3 Cover and shake thoroughly.

4 Strain into the prepared glass.

SUMMER SANGRIA

))HEN YOU THINK "LITERARY BAR," you probably envision a down-and-dirty Irish pub, the sort of place where James Joyce grabbed a pint and some inspiration. But in New York City, even writers enjoy a hip hangout and a little celebrity-owner name-dropping now and again, so here goes: Sebastian Junger, author of The Perfect Storm; Scott Anderson, journalist; Nanette Burstein, Oscar-nominated director of On the Ropes; and Jerome O'Connor, film producer. Owners like these carry serious cool quotient with aspiring writers, and the prospect of chatting with Junger alone is enough to attract folks who wouldn't cross Park Avenue to meet George Clooney or Marky Mark. Even if you don't find Junger, you will discover regular readings by prominent writers, excellent pub fare, such as fish and chips, and a nice selection of intimate seating and tasty cocktails. Forget the Guinness, the house Summer Sangria vanquishes the despair of writer's block in a rainbow of fruit and red wine.

3 ounces red wine

1 ounce fresh orange juice

1 ounce pineapple juice

1 ounce brandy

1 teaspoon sugar

Cubes of fresh mango and watermelon

Splash of ginger ale

Thin slices of grapefruit, oranges,
   lemons, and limes

1 In an ice-filled cocktail shaker, combine the wine, juices,
   brandy, sugar, and fruit cubes. Cover and shake thoroughly.

2 Strain into an ice-filled HIGHBALL GLASS.

3 Top with the ginger ale.

4 Garnish with the citrus slices.

Sangria is seeing a real resurgence. Like so many retro-revivals, this one seems to have been jumpstarted in New York. In fact, Sangria was introduced to the nation in New York, at the Spanish Pavilion at the New York World's Fair of 1964. Although the traditional version is made with red wine, as above, I occasionally use white wine with tropical fruits or even sparkling Spanish cava to add a twist to this always refreshing drink.

POMEGRANATE MARTINI

THE PEN-TOP BAR & TERRACE

WHEN IN POSSESSION OF ONE OF THE BEST ROOFTOP VIEWS in the city, you don't let a little thing like winter stand in the way. And thanks to the recent renovation of The Peninsula, you can now peruse Fifth Avenue from on high in the comfort of the glass-enclosed Pen-Top Bar, complete with illuminated glass counters that change colors almost as often as the lights on the Empire State Building. The bar clientele is mostly patrons of the posh hotel making this a perfect place for stargazing of all types. For a romantic nightcap, I can suggest no better place, and the drink of choice has to be the Pomegranate Martini. Technically it's really nothing more than a Cosmo with pomegranate juice instead of cranberry, but why argue over semantics? Bottom line is, this drink offers a whole new perspective, just like the Pen-Top.

3½ ounces citrus-flavored vodka

½ ounce Cointreau

½ ounce pomegranate juice

¼ ounce fresh lime juice

1 orange twist

1   In an ice-filled cocktail shaker, combine the vodka, Cointreau, and juices.

2   Cover and shake thoroughly.

3   Strain into a chilled **COCKTAIL GLASS.** Garnish with the orange twist.

If you're staying here on the corporate card, I can also suggest the Jewel in a Glass, one of the few cocktails made entirely with wine—but not just any wines: This $75 effervescent gem consists of 1 ounce of Dolce, the sweet wine from California's Far Niente Winery, and 6 ounces of Louis Roederer Champagne Cristal mixed in a chilled champagne flute.

FORGETTING OUR MANNERS

W ATCHING CONSUMMATE BARTENDERS—mixologists, bar chefs, whatever they fancy themselves—prepare cocktails is an especially entertaining treat because these pros not only employ showmanship and theatricality, but they also pay attention to every detail while they perform. Indeed, when there's an expert bartender in the house, the action behind the bar can be a sideshow to the action throughout the rest of the place.

Such craftsmanship was once the norm at just about every bar in town. In 1912, Charles Mahoney outlined the marks of a great bartender in the Hoffman House Bartending Guide. He claimed that a bar's atmosphere was provided almost exclusively by the bartenders, whose "temperament, disposition, and magnetism have a lot to do with it." The high level of service he described was in keeping with the usual expectations for bar service in the early twentieth century. Bartenders used silver tongs rather than bare hands to add garnishes to drinks and often wore white pressed coats (as at Monteaux Café, 1902, below).

Sadly, the craftsmanship of making cocktails suffered disastrously in this country during Prohibition when bars went either underground or belly-up. When was the last time you watched a bartender polish your glass with a white linen towel before she pours your drink into it? Few bar patrons can remember a time when such nuances were typical, but this brand of service can still be seen regularly in Europe. Although Americans taught the Europeans how to make cocktails in the first place, the Euros kept our traditions alive while our parents and grandparents were siphoning gin out of the bathtub for thirteen utterly embarrassing years. After Prohibition was repealed, an entire generation of Americans basically forgot what all the fuss was about. Let's hope we're getting back on track now.

RED CAT DARK 'N STORMY

*D*ESPITE THE SUCCESSES OF THE HARRISON and The Mermaid Inn, co-owners Danny Abrams and chef Jimmy Bradley's inaugural effort The Red Cat is still my favorite. From the second I stepped into the entryway bar I was struck by how comfortable the room is, while feeling au courant at the same time. I thought, "This is the sort of place where I could happily park it and throw down a few drinks without losing my shirt." It's the sort of place you immediately know you'll return to again and again, and I have. The bar offers twists on classic cocktails, like the Bermudian national drink, Dark 'n Stormy. The name of this drink is copyrighted by Goslings, so technically you have to use their luscious dark rum. But, really, why would you use anything else? The real key to this drink, however, is ginger beer—not ginger ale. Ginger beer, more renowned for its role in the far less exciting Moscow Mule cocktail, offers a little heat over its pop counterpart. And Red Cat adds to the effect with a touch of Chinese fire.

2 ounces Gosling's Black Seal Rum
1 tablespoon fresh ginger juice
1 pinch ground Szechuan peppercorns
1 squeeze of fresh lime juice
6 ounces ginger beer
1 lemon wheel

1 In an ice-filled cocktail shaker, combine the rum, ginger juice, Szechuan pepper, and lime juice, adjusting lime and pepper to taste.

2 Cover and shake thoroughly.

3 Strain into a double ROCKS GLASS filled with ice.

4 Top with the ginger beer. Garnish with the lemon wheel.

True ginger beer is fermented with yeast, just like real beer, but has the alcohol removed. It's no surprise then that one of my favorites, with its mouth-warming jolt of ginger, comes from Desnoes & Geddes, the makers of Red Stripe beer in Jamaica. With the diversity of Caribbean immigrants in New York City, you should have no trouble finding a selection of ginger beers at the corner bodega. Szechuan peppercorns can be difficult to find as importing them is currently prohibited due to the USDA's worry about their harboring harmful plant diseases. You may be able to find them in Asian markets if you ask; otherwise substitute regular black peppercorns.

PEAR MARTINI

BLUE RIBBON

ALTHOUGH THERE ARE NOW FIVE BLUE RIBBON RESTAURANTS in New York City, I still like the original one on Sullivan Street best. The bar itself is one of the smallest in town, but I'd bet it sees a lot more action than many bars twice its size. Back in my bachelor days a decade ago, I'd bring dates to this chic-but-casual eatery, jockey for a seat at the bar, and let barman James Shrum dazzle us with cocktails while the master shucker opened oysters with unfettered aplomb. Ten years later, James is still there, and the drinks are as dazzling as I remember. The classic Martini is still king here when it comes to cocktails neutral enough to complement the raw seafood, but a taste of a pear-infused concoction recently got my attention because its sweet floral notes were beautifully balanced with acidity. The acidity is both necessary and logical with the crawfish, crabs, oysters, and clams perched in the mountain of ice at the end of the bar.

Although Blue Ribbon's Pear Martini calls for Belle de Brillet, you could, in a pinch, substitute any pear-flavored brandy or schnapps. However, if you do, don't expect the drink to have the same finesse that comes from this beautiful brandy.

2 ounces Belle de Brillet

1 ounce Absolut Citron

1 ounce fresh lime juice

1 In an ice-filled cocktail shaker, combine all ingredients.

2 Cover and shake thoroughly.

3 Strain into a chilled **COCKTAIL GLASS.**

As soon as Belle de Brillet hits the glass you'll smell the pears in this fabulous French liqueur, as if they were freshly squeezed into the bottle. Keep sniffing—gentle now—and you'll smell the fiery vanilla aromas of Brillet Cognac in the background. This concoction is the brainchild of Jean-Louis Brillet, blending ripe Alsatian pears with his beautiful Cognac. With this potent a pear aroma you must be wondering how many it takes to keep the Cognac in check. The answer is a whopping twenty-two pounds per bottle.

PISCO SOUR

A T THIS LOWER EAST SIDE NUEVO LATINO BISTRO, which borrows its name from the tiny household restaurants of Cuba, the seafood-heavy menu of chef Aaron Sanchez is accompanied by fabulous cocktails with a similarly Latin slant. The El Vampiro margarita benefits from an addition of hibiscus flower juice and a spicy rim of salt and cayenne pepper. And the refreshing Mexican rice drink horchata, with its sweet cinnamon and cloves, is especially tasty with a shot of Bacardi. Even better are the prices: cocktails cost about half of what you'd pay for the same drinks in a swank hotel bar, and they're halved again daily during Happy Hour. For a rarely seen classic, be sure to give the Pisco Sour a try. This may look similar to your usual Caipirinha or Mojito, but the addition of egg white adds a beautiful, light frothiness to the distinctive flavor of pisco.

1 heaping teaspoon sugar (or to taste)
1 lime, cut into quarters
1½ ounces pisco
1 egg white
2 ounces club soda
Dash of bitters

1 In a cocktail shaker, muddle together the sugar and lime.

2 Add the pisco and egg white, and ice.

3 Cover and shake vigorously.

4 Strain into a chilled **COCKTAIL GLASS.**

5 Top with the club soda and a dash of bitters.

Pisco is Peruvian sugarcane brandy, and while the popularity of this cocktail has fallen in the U.S. since its heyday in the 1940s, it remains a source of national pride in both Peru and Chile. Traditionally, the drink is served much stronger, using about another ounce of pisco in a comparable recipe. But Paladar's nicely tempered version suits me fine. Note that the recipe calls for raw egg white. The American Egg Board advises against consuming any raw egg products. However, whites pose a much lesser risk than yolks.

THE BIGGER APPLE MARTINI

FIFTY SEVEN FIFTY SEVEN BAR

*F*RIENDS OF MINE GRIPE ABOUT THE PRICES of cocktails here, but what they don't seem to realize is that you really get two for one. Each impeccably made cocktail is poured from a shaker or carafe that's left nearby to refresh your drink and keep it properly cold. On particularly slow days I've milked one of those shakers for an hour before ordering another, and that seems incongruously generous in this grand, bustling space. But the bountiful libations are actually perfectly in scale with architect I. M. Pei's monumental space: soaring ceilings, wall-sized windows, and plenty of small tables for solo contemplation or cozy canoodling. Crisply dressed waiters deliver complimentary nibbles, and proffer a cocktail list that changes often but never strays too far from the classics, interspersed with the flavors du jour, proving that a place can be both classy and trendy without being trite. Which is why I love The Bigger Apple Martini—because it represents both the style and scale of this place in perfect balance.

This recipe calls for green apple puree, which you can make at home if you're ambitious: peel and core a green apple; and puree it in a food processor with a few ounces of simple syrup—just enough to form a smooth liquid. This will last in the fridge for several days in a covered container (you could even freeze it to reuse later). Of course you could substitute with apple-flavored brandy, but you'd never get the grainy texture that the real deal imparts.

3 ounces apple-flavored vodka
1 ounce green apple puree (see Tip)
½ ounce fresh sour mix
1 slice of green apple
Dried cranberries

1 Into an ice-filled cocktail shaker combine the vodka, apple puree, and sour mix.

2 Cover and shake vigorously.

3 Strain into a chilled **COCKTAIL GLASS.**

4 Garnish with apple slice and accompany with dried cranberries on the side.

PARADISE MARTINI

CUB ROOM

*T*HIS STYLISH SoHo RESTAURANT AND BAR takes its name from the inner sanctum of Sherman Billingsley's legendary Stork Club, located on East 53rd Street in Manhattan. In his 1948 book *Where to Eat in New York*, Robert W. Dana observed that the place was frequented by all the hottest celebrities and politicians, and the Cub Room's Table 50 was "probably the most photographed table in the world." So our modern-day Cub Room has high aspirations. The place pays further homage by offering a Stork Club classic cocktail, the Paradise Martini, in "its original form." With vodka? Sorry, but no. Vodka was virtually unknown when Bing Crosby was sipping here. Sure enough, after consulting my original edition of *The Stork Club Bar Book*, I can confirm that the Cub Room has succumbed to the sin of substituting vodka for our Prohibition pal, gin. Still, it's a tasty and well-crafted drink, so much so that I hope this Cub Room, like the original, sticks around for another 40 years.

While cocktail and food pairing is now de rigueur, it's really nothing new. The Stork Club recommended enjoying the Paradise before their famous fish dishes. And if you want to truly taste the original, simply alter your ingredients to 1¾ ounces gin, ¾ ounce apricot brandy, and ¾ ounce orange juice. Now that's a cocktail!

2 ounces Belvedere Vodka
1 ounce apricot brandy
1 ounce apricot puree

1 Combine the vodka, liqueur, and puree in a cocktail shaker filled with ice.

2 Stir vigorously.

3 Strain into a chilled COCKTAIL GLASS.

APRICOT PUREE

½ cup peeled, chopped fresh apricots
1 tablespoon triple sec
1 tablespoon simple syrup

Combine the apricots, triple sec, and syrup in a small food processor or blender. Process until smooth.

CUB ROOM
NEW YORK

CAIPIRINHA

COPACABANA

HE COPA IS MOST DEFINITELY THE GREAT-GRANDDADDY of Manhattan dance clubs, as it's been open almost nonstop since 1940, albeit in three different locations. The latest locale, which opened in 2002, is twice the size of the club that inspired Barry Manilow; in fact it's nothing short of massive, with music and dancing on two levels. Downstairs in the Copa Room, a DJ pumps out mostly hip-hop, while upstairs in the enormous Carmen Miranda Room live bands play salsa and merengue for teeming crowds. And when I say crowds, I mean 3,400 at maximum capacity, many coming for the Tuesday night "After Work Party." I'd like to think that a good number of people come here for the cocktails, especially the Caipirinha, which is a nod to the Brazilian beach that gives this club its name, but I suspect the free buffet on Tuesdays has a lot to do with it, too. Although I must admit it's a very good buffet indeed.

Cachaça, also known as aguardiente, is a Brazilian spirit distilled from sugarcane juice. Although parallels are often drawn between cachaça and rum, rum is distilled from molasses, while cachaça is distilled directly from the unrefined juice of sugarcane. Before the juice is distilled, it's fermented in a wooden or copper container for three weeks, then boiled down three times into a concentrate. It has an aroma similar to rum, but is quite different in flavor.

1 lime cut into 8 small wedges
2 teaspoons superfine sugar
2½ ounces cachaça

1 Drop the lime wedges into a **ROCKS GLASS,** and gently mash them.

2 Add the sugar and muddle until it dissolves into the lime juice.

3 Add ice.

4 Top with cachaça, and stir.

My parents, who grew up just across the Hudson in Jersey City, have memories of going into the Big City for fun at the original Copacabana (when it was located on East 60th Street), but their recollections are considerably—and typically—divergent. Mom remembers going for the first time with my dad after their senior prom in 1959. "Our prom was at the Hotel Statler [now the Hotel Pennsylvania], and afterwards we went to the Latin Quarter for drinks and a show, and then we went for nightcaps at the Copacabana, because that was the thing to do." Fast-forward a decade and Dad recalls a different kind of beautiful evening at the Copa when Mom, by now a mother of three, talked him into taking her to see Tom Jones. "You had to see this: All the women were standing on the tables, taking off their panties and throwing them at Jones. Who knows what your mother would have done if I weren't there!"

NEW YORK SOUR

*S*CHILLER'S LIQUOR BAR, restaurateur extraordinaire Keith McNally's latest venture, may share design elements that bring to mind siblings Balthazar and Pastis—cracked-glaze subway tiles and faux-aged mirrors—but Schiller's is more like McNally's Pravda, where the accent is more on spirits than wine—hence the "Liquor Bar" moniker. Not surprisingly, McNally imported Pravda's master mixologist Dushan Zaric here as head bartender to create a list of drinks that would make Jerry Thomas, father of American cocktaildom, beam with pride. In fact, Zaric pays homage to Thomas with his Jerry Thomas Manhattan, which, the menu notes, is slightly different and more exciting than today's standard Manhattan. Indeed it is, but my favorite cocktail in this raucous restaurant is Zaric's New York Sour, which on paper reads like the merging of a classic sour with sangria, but in the glass is a brilliant balance of red wine fruit with mouthwatering sour crispness. Sort of like biting into a ripe McIntosh apple.

2 ounces blended whiskey

1 ounce fresh lemon juice

¾ ounce simple syrup

Splash of fresh orange juice

¾ ounce red wine

1 orange wheel

1 maraschino cherry

1 In a cocktail shaker, combine the whiskey, lemon juice, syrup, and orange juice.

2 Add ice, cover, and shake well, up to 10 seconds.

3 Strain into an ice-filled **ROCKS GLASS.**

4 Float the wine on top.

5 Garnish with the orange wheel and maraschino cherry.

The New York Sour calls for red wine, so consider a dry, fruity red, such as a pinot noir, merlot, or shiraz. Whatever you do, do not use "White Zinfandel" or anything labeled "cooking wine"— it's not that kind of recipe.

LYCHEE BELLINI

LE COLONIAL

*T*HIS RESTAURANT EVOKES THE ROMANCE OF VIETNAM'S French colonial era in the 1920s and '30s. With wicker furniture and the soft breeze of slowly spinning ceiling fans, it's got a film noir allure. The prices are modest for the excellent quality of the Asian cuisine, heavy on seafood and offering excellent standards like Cha Gio—spring rolls of shrimp, pork, and mushrooms. After ten years, Le Colonial remains frozen in time, having lost none of its luster. They've chosen to celebrate the anniversary with a wonderfully aromatic twist on the Bellini, made with canned lychees. Interestingly, the peach—pureed for the original Bellini at Harry's Bar in Venice—was, like the lychee, first cultivated in China. Both are now grown throughout the world and do particularly well in the southern U.S., so you can always experiment with fresh lychees if you like. The natural sweetness makes it perfect with spicy, exotic Asian foods.

Many wine lovers identify the flavor of lychee fruit in gewürztraminer, a German wine grape, as well in some chardonnays. The combination of this aromatic, juicy fruit with Champagne makes it the perfect cocktail to sway your oenophile friends. If you can't find a fresh lychee nut, just reserve one from the can.

1 (8 ounce) can lychees in syrup

3 ounces Champagne

1 fresh lychee nut

1 Place the canned lychees with their syrup into a blender and process to a smooth puree.

2 Chill the lychee puree.

3 Combine 3 ounces of the lychee puree in a **CHAMPAGNE FLUTE** with an equal amount of Champagne.

4 Garnish with a whole lychee nut.

Chapter 3

COSMO CAPITAL

CRYSTAL COSMO

AQUABITE

8½ TANGERINE COSMO

NOT-SO-COSMOPOLITAN

SPARKLY COSMO

COSMO FOR TWO

METROPOLITAN

CRYSTAL COSMO

*T*UCKED INTO A CORNER OF THE LUXURIOUS HÔTEL PLAZA ATHÉNÉE, Bar Seine is not so much timeless as it is transformative: It feels like Paris. So much so, in fact, television producers have taped scenes here as if it really *were* Paris. Practically everyone here seems to order Cosmopolitans — but they don't look anything like the typical rose-colored concoctions that are found just about everywhere else. They are clear, crystal clear, as the name implies, and that's the idea the folks at Bar Seine had in mind when they put a spin on the real deal. The trick, of course, is white cranberry juice, which lends the drink the viscosity of fruit juice without tinting it in the least. Frankly, it looks like a Martini, and perfectly sophisticated, too, in this exotic room, which I believe boasts the only leather floor in Manhattan.

Bar Seine's Crystal Cosmo uses white cranberry juice, but you could use the red variety if you can't find the white. What really matters is that you make sure the glass is well chilled, as the condensation on the glass will make the drink's clarity shimmer beautifully.

2 ounces Absolut Citron

½ ounce Cointreau

1 ounce white cranberry juice

1 lime wedge

1 In an ice-filled cocktail shaker, combine the vodka, Cointreau, and juice.

2 Cover and shake thoroughly.

3 Strain into chilled **COCKTAIL GLASS.**

4 Garnish with the lime wedge.

AQUABITE

AQUAGRILL

HE SHELLFISH THEME IN THIS LOVELY, PALE-YELLOW DINING ROOM is so complete—they decorate the light fixtures and are used to make life-size representations of crustaceans on the walls—the beautifully arranged mollusks adorning the bar look like part of the décor. Thankfully, they're not, as the shucker skillfully proves, opening hundreds of oysters every day to the delight of barflies like me. While there's no denying that most people here come for chef-owner Jeremy Marshall's masterful husbandry of fish, folks like me come to sit at the comfortable, neighborhoody bar and chat with Marshall's wife, Jennifer, who runs the front of the house and has a way of describing oysters that keeps me coming back. She also has a hand in what's poured here, and created the Aquabite to showcase vodka's affinity with oysters, especially when kissed with a splash of citrus—which is exactly how I like my oysters, and my cocktails, too.

Try serving the drink in stemless short glasses set in a bowl of ice alongside raw oysters or clams in their shells.

1½ ounces vodka
½ ounce triple sec
Splash of cranberry juice
Splash of fresh grapefruit juice
Splash of fresh lime juice
1 lime twist

1 Into an ice-filled cocktail shaker, pour all liquid ingredients.

2 Cover and shake thoroughly.

3 Strain into a chilled COCKTAIL GLASS. Garnish with a lime twist.

It must be a "Dad" thing when it comes to not parting with shucked shells. My father, Tony, saves all of the thousands of mussel, clam, and oyster shells he amasses during summer entertaining, to decorate the flowerbeds that border my parents' "compound"—a family joke referring to the polar-opposite riches of another Italian family, the Corleones of The Godfather fame. Jeremy Marshall's dad, Mel, uses his plethora of mollusk shells to create mesmerizing patterns on canvas, including the ones that adorn the walls at Aqua-grill's bar. While many restaurants employ artwork as quiet background, Marshall's vibrant creations are worth seeking out for both their novelty and whimsy.

8½ TANGERINE COSMO

*I*T'S NO SURPRISE TO ME that the semicircular, tangerine-carpeted Italian-wedding staircase is exactly the same shade as my nuclear-colored cocktail at this ever-trendy subterranean restaurant. Of course, it's no coincidence that Brasserie 8½ created a drink—grafted upon on the most popular cocktail on the planet—that matches the décor. The Brasserie 8½ Cosmo captures the energy of this bustling brasserie: it's trendy, but au courant cool—even though it's no longer the new kid on the block, and very different from its even-cooler sibling, Brasserie, a few blocks away. What I like about this Cosmo is that it balances fresh citrus fruit with a touch of sweetness, which keeps it refreshing without being the least bit cloying. That makes it perfect to pair with Chef Julian Alonzo's Crispy Calamari with Meyer lemon remoulade or Coconut Shrimp with honey mustard oil.

2 ounces Absolut Mandrin

1 ounce Cointreau

½ ounce fresh tangerine juice

½ ounce fresh lime juice

½ ounce simple syrup

1 tangerine or orange wedge

1 In an ice-filled cocktail shaker combine all the ingredients except the fruit wedge.

2 Shake thoroughly.

3 Strain into a chilled **COCKTAIL GLASS.** Garnish with the wedge of either tangerine or orange.

Fresh tangerines are usually available only from October through May, making it pretty difficult to make this drink in summer—when it is especially refreshing. A good substitute would be somewhat-hard-to-find bottled juice (check out organic grocery shops). If you can't find fresh or bottled, a combination of cranberry and orange juice in equal parts works quite well.

NOT-SO-COSMOPOLITAN

R M

*T*HE MOMENT I SAW THIS DRINK ON THE COCKTAIL MENU at the plush RM, I knew it had to be an "insider" jab at the glitterati by chef/co-owner Rick Moonen. Moonen, a native New Yorker who would have you believe he's shy and well mannered, is also a bad-boy nuyawker who would have no problem flipping the bird at chichi Cosmo drinkers. In other words, being a New Yorker has nothing to do with being cosmopolitan. And while this cocktail is based on the Cosmo's foundation, it strays off the common riff with the addition of passion fruit puree, which when combined with another twist, blue curaçao, turns the drink a funky green. In fact, it's sort of the color of both our Hudson and East Rivers; perhaps an allusion to the seafood fare that thankfully is caught far from our shores. Otherwise, Moonen's Seared Coriander-crusted Yellowtail with Tangerine, Avocado, and Cinnamon Oil wouldn't taste nearly as good. Conversely, the water in the ice cubes used to make this cocktail is as local as Moonen, and makes the drinks taste just fine.

2 ounces citrus-flavored vodka

1 ounce Cointreau

1 ounce white cranberry juice

½ ounce fresh lime juice

½ ounce simple syrup

¾ ounce passion fruit puree

Dash of blue curaçao

Slice of star fruit

1 In an ice-filled cocktail shaker, combine the vodka, Cointreau, juices, syrup, puree, and curaçao.

2 Shake vigorously.

3 Strain into a chilled **COCKTAIL GLASS.**

4 Garnish with the star fruit.

RM's twist on the Cosmo calls for Cointreau instead of lowly triple sec, but you could of course substitute the latter for the former. Essential to achieving its lovely shade of green, however, is the blue curaçao, which isn't expensive by any means, and good to have on hand when experimenting with colorful cocktails.

SPARKLY COSMO

*E*VERYTHING SPARKLES AT THE REGENCY—a Loews Hotel—from the marble and gilt bathrooms, to the bejeweled patrons, and even the pink drinks. After decades of catering to the well-heeled, The Regency obviously subscribes to one of my tenets of entertaining: Champagne makes everything, and everyone, infinitely more interesting. Even our tired cocktail companion the Cosmopolitan looks like it's fresh from Botox when doused with a little bubbly. While The Regency offers several lounge options (the most famous of which is the somewhat pricey supper club Feinstein's At The Regency, renowned for its cabaret acts), I actually prefer the quiet solitude of a couch in The Library. Here one can almost imagine Princess Grace sweeping through the lobby, or hear Audrey Hepburn's laugh echoing through the miles of marble.

In addition to Cointreau, not mere triple sec, the hallmark of the Cosmopolitan is good citrus vodka. Absolut Citron and Ketel One Citroen are still the staples. But with the ever-growing number of flavored brands, you can feel free to substitute a favorite such as Belvedere Cytrus or Grey Goose Vodka L'Orange.

1 ounce Ketel One Citroen
½ ounce Cointreau
1 ounce cranberry juice
⅛ ounce fresh lime juice
2 ounces Champagne Perrier-Jouët
1 lime wedge

1 Combine the vodka, Cointreau, and juices in a cocktail shaker with ice.

2 Cover and shake vigorously.

3 Strain into a chilled COCKTAIL GLASS.

4 Top with the Champagne.

5 Garnish with the wedge of lime.

COSMO FOR TWO

*W*HEN I ENTER A BAR, I don't want to think immediately about leaving. But that's the nature of the theater district, and as an institution among theatergoers and actors alike, Sardi's is always operating on that invisible countdown to showtime. Everything is old school, from the staff to the menu (Baked Alaska, anyone?) to the décor, which consists of hundreds of caricatures that make for great entertainment over a hit-and-run dinner. I'm certain my near-sighted Nana could beat me two for one in the celebrity name game here. But it's this history, and the staff's polished poise in hustling you out without rushing you, that makes Sardi's a perennial theater favorite. In the interest of time, I'd recommend ordering the Cosmo that serves two. It's a riff on the classic, with the addition of vermouth giving it an old-school feel, which is apropos here. Ask the bartender to hail your cab while the drink is still pouring, and you're on your way to a matinee. Now that's efficiency.

½ ounce dry vermouth

2½ ounce Cointreau

6 ounces vodka

½ cup cranberry juice

Juice of ½ lime

2 lime twists

1 Combine the vermouth, Cointreau, vodka, and cranberry juice in an ice-filled cocktail shaker.

2 Cover and shake vigorously.

3 Add the lime juice, stir, and strain into two chilled **COCKTAIL GLASSES.**

4 Garnish with a twist.

Want to operate with the speed of Sardi's? For your next party, consider batching any of our cocktail recipes in advance and keeping them in a cooler with a spout. Before serving, just tap and shake or stir with ice as required. Just don't mix cocktails containing fresh citrus juice more than a day ahead.

METROPOLITAN
MARION'S CONTINENTAL RESTAURANT & LOUNGE

WHILE COMPETING IN PARIS as a member of the Hungarian Swim Team in the World Peace Games, Marion Nagy seized the opportunity to flee from Stalinist Budapest. After a successful modeling career in Paris, she eventually made her way to New York City and, in 1950, opened Marion's Continental Restaurant & Lounge. Located on the Bowery, Marion's recalls its heyday by hosting fashion brunches for upcoming designers as well as one of the longest-running burlesque shows in Manhattan—the Pontani Sisters. Of course, you're just as likely to catch some quality cross-dressing any night of the week as the locals mix it up with one of the occasional celebrities whose names are recorded on autographed plates. Marion's, however, gets its footnote in cocktail history for the Metropolitan. Unable to bring himself to mix one more Cosmopolitan, bartender Chuck Coggins mixed one with Absolut Kurant, dubbing it the Metropolitan. It's the Cosmo in drag: strangely alluring, but you can sense something's not quite right.

If you take out the cranberry juice from the Metropolitan and use plain vodka, you'll have the classic kamikaze, named after the Japanese suicide bombers of World War II. It can be served in a cocktail glass or over ice in an old-fashioned glass, but beware: the kamikaze can go down all too easily.

3 ounces Absolut Kurant
2 ounces triple sec
1 ounce fresh lime juice
Splash of cranberry juice
1 lime wedge

1 In an ice-filled cocktail shaker, combine the vodka, triple sec, and juices.

2 Cover and shake thoroughly.

3 Strain into a chilled **COCKTAIL GLASS**.

4 Garnish with the lime wedge.

In Behind Bars (2004), former bartender Ty Wenzel chronicles her tales of bartending in New York City, most of which come from her decade-long stint at Marion's. Among the revelations: every flirtatious, cute bartender I ever met just wanted my fat tip. In retrospect, I still don't care.

Chapter 4

MIXOLOGIST MADE

CHERRY SMASH

CHUCUMBER COCKTAIL

TABLATINI

TANTRIS SIDECAR

PARADISO

THE GOLD RUSH

INDIAN ROSE

PARIS, NEW JERSEY

'SANS'GRIA BLANCO

THE SHINING STAR

PRICKLY PEAR MARGARITA

CHERRY SMASH

ASTER MIXOLOGIST JULIE REINER'S FLATIRON LOUNGE is a tribute to the classic cocktail, set in a historic building dating back to the Roaring Twenties. Although this room—featuring a thirty-foot-long Art Deco counter from the legendary Manhattan Ballroom—feels old and well worn, it opened just in 2003. Already, however, it seems to have become as classic as the cocktails served here. Reiner, who's been working in the bar biz for 18 years, sought to create a bar where the focus was on properly made, unadulterated cocktails served by consummate pros; all of whom she personally trains. "Everything's fresh and the cocktails are the stars," she says modestly. The drinks are exquisite, and offered in flights, such as the "Flight Back in Time," spotlighting Rat Pack–era favorites such as the Sidecar, the Sazerac, and the Aviation cocktail. One of Reiner's favorites, however, is the Cherry Smash, inspired by her discovery of Edelkirsch, a beautiful cherry liqueur.

4 brandied cherries (see Tip)

¼ ounce Edelkirsch

1½ ounces Courvoisier V.S.

½ ounce fresh lemon juice

1 ounce orange curaçao

1 In an ice-filled cocktail shaker, muddle 2 of the cherries.

2 Add Edelkirsch, Courvoisier, lemon juice, and curaçao.

3 Shake thoroughly, and then strain into a chilled COCKTAIL GLASS. Garnish with the remaining 2 brandied cherries.

BRANDIED CHERRIES

2 pounds dark, sweet cherries

⅓ cup sugar

⅓ cup water

1 tablespoon lemon juice

½ cup brandy

Wash and pit cherries. Combine sugar, water, and lemon juice in a large, nonreactive pot. Bring to a boil; reduce heat to a simmer. Add cherries and simmer until hot. Remove from heat; stir in brandy. This recipe yields about 2 pints. Cherries will keep, covered in a jar in the refrigerator, for at least a month. They also make a great garnish for Manhattans and just about any drink that calls for a cherry.

Mixologist Julie Reiner prefers to use Marie Brizard Orange Curaçao because of its intense, real-orange flavor. Both the brandied cherries and Edelkirsch could involve trips to specialty stores, but are both must-haves for this recipe. Reiner suggests that if dark, sweet cherries are in season, you should make the brandied cherries from scratch.

CHUCUMBER COCKTAIL

*T*HE STORY BEHIND THE MULTICULTI VIBE at Sushi Samba's two New York City locations is inspired by the twentieth-century migration of Japanese fortune hunters to South America's coffee plantations in Peru and Brazil, a cultural phenomenon that launched a culinary coup—and a restaurant concept to boot. That's how we get hearty moquecas (savory seafood stews cooked in palm oil) and colorful seviches alongside simple miso soup and silky sashimi. Cocktails here aspire to similar comminglings of ethnic liqueurs, which is how we find a cocktail list pairing a vodka-like Japanese distillate called shochu with spirits and liqueurs from around the globe. The most striking combination, in my opinion, is the Chucumber, made with shochu and fresh cucumbers, which balance the sweetness of Licor 43 (a.k.a. Cuarenta Y Tres), a vanilla-flavored liqueur whose origins allegedly go back to around 200 B.C. and which contains at least 43 ingredients, mainly fruits and herbs.

The foundation of Sushi Samba's "Chucumber" is shochu, which you should be able to find at liquor stores with considerable inventories. Three that are readily available in this country: Takara Jun Shochu, Yokaichi Kome Shochu, and Yokaichi Mugi Shochu, all three of which were priced around $18.

4 cucumber wheels, peeled
½ teaspoon sugar
½ ounce fresh lime juice
½ ounce Licor 43 (Cuarenta Y Tres)
2 ounces shochu

1 In a cocktail shaker, muddle 3 of the cucumber wheels with the sugar and lime juice.

2 Add the Licor 43 and shochu and top with ice.

3 Cover and shake thoroughly.

4 Strain into a chilled **COCKTAIL GLASS.** Garnish with the remaining cucumber wheel.

SUSHI SAMBA

Sushi Samba Beverage Director Paul Tanguay is a sommelier who has always been fascinated by sake, which led him to discover shochu, a Japanese distillate that he describes as something between vodka and a sake. It's very much like a flavorful vodka (but only 50-proof), and reminiscent of sake—which is made by fermenting rice, while shochu can be made by distilling barley, rice, sweet potato, or sugar cane. Although it smells very much like sake—think overripe melon—Tanguay says that the scent comes from koji, an enzyme that converts starches to sugars in both sake and shochu. But that's where the similarities end. Shochu originates from the island of Kyushu and the western part of the island of Honshu, which are significantly warmer than the rest of Japan, and therefore difficult regions for brewing sake—hence the use of distillation. And because shochu isn't limited to rice, its flavor profile runs the gamut from crisp and light (rice) to peaty, earthy, and strong (potato).

TABLATINI

*T*HE LUSH, CURVILINEAR BREAD BAR on the first floor at Tabla, which hugs the sweeping semicircular staircase leading to the formal dining room, shares a convivial tavern feel that owner Danny Meyer seems to have down pat, the benchmark being his Gramercy Tavern. Here, Meyer has installed chef Floyd Cardoz to create innovative cuisine based on the tastes and traditions of Cardoz's native India, filtered through the lens of his formal European training. The Bread Bar feels relaxed and comfortable, well-worn in since its crazy opening mobs a few years back, and it's in the foreground of the tandoor ovens where cooks crank out fresh *naan* bread. The signature cocktail here, the Tablatini, was inspired by a pastry chef's contribution to a cocktail "creative session" —a batch of lemongrass-infused pineapple "soup." The bar team added a splash of citrus-flavored vodka to the soup and a house drink was born. Try it with Cardoz's crab cakes in a crisp papadum shell.

Lemongrass-infused pineapple juice is certainly something you won't find in any supermarket. However, it's relatively easy to make if you have fresh lemongrass on hand—which you can find at any good Asian grocery. To make this infusion, bring 8 ounces of either fresh or canned pineapple juice to a boil. Turn off heat and steep 4 stalks of lemongrass, tied together, for at least 15 minutes, longer if desired. Cool and store in refrigerator for up to a week.

2 ounces Ketel One Citroen
2 ounces lemongrass-infused pineapple juice (see Tip)
Splash of fresh lime juice
1 fresh pineapple chunk
1 lemongrass stick (optional)

1 In an ice-filled cocktail shaker, combine the vodka and juices.

2 Cover and shake thoroughly.

3 Strain into a chilled COCKTAIL GLASS.

4 Garnish with the fresh pineapple chunk on the rim, with lemongrass skewer if you like.

TANTRIS SIDECAR

Bemelmans Bar is one of the City's few remaining piano bars, a place where the tinkling of the ivories strikes perfect harmony with the clinking of ice cubes. A recent renovation restored this bastion of Old New York, located in The Carlyle hotel, to its full glory. Dale DeGroff, King Cocktail himself, was behind the revitalized bar program, and his prodigy Audrey Saunders now shakes up her own brand of libations with a nod to the classics. Referring to her Tantris Sidecar, which adds pineapple and Green Chartreuse to the original, Saunders says, "I just love this recipe—it has much more depth and complexity than the classic recipe, as well as a new modern edge." But beyond the cocktails, not much has changed about Bemelmans Bar. Well-heeled Upper East Siders still sip and delight in the whimsical murals by former Carlyle resident Ludwig Bemelmans. Gentleman, don your jacket and tie, and no one should come without a credit card. The piano player takes requests, but romance like this doesn't come cheap.

1 ounce Hennessy V.S.
½ ounce Busnel Calvados
½ ounce Cointreau
½ ounce fresh lemon juice
½ ounce simple syrup
¼ ounce pineapple juice
¼ ounce Green Chartreuse
Granulated sugar
1 lemon twist

1 Chill a COCKTAIL GLASS with ice and water.

2 In an ice-filled cocktail shaker, combine the liquid ingredients.

3 Cover and shake thoroughly.

4 Empty the water from the chilled cocktail glass and coat the rim by dipping it in sugar.

5 Strain the cocktail into the prepared glass.

6 Garnish with the lemon twist.

Though there are a number of green drinks out there, from apple Martinis to grasshoppers, there is only one naturally green liqueur. Green Chartreuse was invented in a French monastery centuries ago. Its recipe, still a closely guarded secret, consists of 130 different plants and involves a precise system of blending and distillation as well as aging in oak casks. The equally enigmatic Yellow Chartreuse is much subtler, but Green Chartreuse is strong and aromatic, so even a small amount can shape the flavor of a cocktail.

Ludwig Bemelmans, author and illustrator, was born in Austria on April 27, 1898. But like so many artists, Bemelmans made New York City his adopted home. His most famous creation is children's book heroine Madeline, a smashing success since her debut in 1939. Madeline went on to visit London and frolic with gypsies, but presumably she never set foot in a bar—unlike Bemelmans, who painted the murals in the bar that now bears his name in exchange for an extended stay at The Carlyle in 1947. The paintings remain as the only public display of his work.

PARADISO

*T*HOUGH THE PARADISO COCKTAIL HERE sounds more heavenly than hellish, Level V's subterranean location coupled with its Middle Ages décor seems more in line with Dante's Inferno. But it's all part of the look, and you can bet it was all painstakingly conceptualized by Stephen Hanson's BR Guest Restaurants, whose other dozen hotspots include Dos Caminos, Blue Fin, and Blue Water Grill. Located underneath Vento Trattoria, this cavernous space has seen many incarnations: It was a factory turned Civil War hospital in the mid-nineteenth century; used as stables for carriage horses at the turn of the twentieth; and for a while toward the turn of the twenty-first was an S&M club called the Vault. Now, Level V (and that's the letter v, not Roman numeral V) serves as both a waiting room for diners and a late-night haunt for revelers looking to pick up or hang with their homeys in one of the private alcoves, replete with bottle service and a sound system that allows you to plug in your iPod. The drinks here are creative, to say the least—departing from classics in content, but not in concept or preparation.

1½ ounces golden rum
½ ounce Lazzaroni Amaretto
1 ounce fresh sour mix
½ ounce white peach puree

1 In a cocktail shaker combine all ingredients.

2 Fill with ice, cover, and shake well.

3 Strain into a chilled COCKTAIL GLASS.

The bar director at Level V recommends Lazzaroni Amaretto in his Paradiso, which raises the question: What the heck is amaretto anyway? Well, technically, it's an almond-flavored liqueur made from apricot pits—yes, apricot pits. That's what makes this otherwise sweet sipper stand out among its toothaching siblings: it's balanced with a bitter-nutty flavor that finishes dry on the palate. White peach puree can be bought frozen or made simply by pureeing fresh, peeled whole peaches when available.

THE GOLD RUSH

*N*AMED FOR THE NEARBY MANHATTAN NEIGHBORHOOD, immortalized most recently by Martin Scorsese's Gangs of New York, this restaurant couldn't be more removed from the chaos and thuggery that ruled these streets over a century ago. A trickling Japanese Zen garden–style fountain sets the mood for the dining room. And hearty pastas and roasted clams feature the homey flavors of a wood-burning fire. Thankfully, bartender Jim Meehan has appropriated a favorite drink from Milk & Honey, a discreet Downtown speakeasy-style bar that makes some of the best drinks in the city. I say thankfully because that bar is so elusive it declined to be included in this book. However, at Five Points, you can enjoy a version of The Gold Rush, basically a whiskey sour with a hint of honey. Five Points's food is worth seeking out and, frankly, this drink is as close as most ever get to the land of Milk & Honey.

To make honey water, combine 5 ounces of honey and 3 ounces of hot, not boiling, water in an 8-ounce squeeze bottle. Stir until the honey dissolves. You'll have a honey simple syrup that combines easily in your drinks.

2½ ounces Maker's Mark
1 ounce fresh lemon juice
1 ounce simple syrup
½ ounce honey water

1 Combine the bourbon, juice, syrup, and honey water in a cocktail shaker with ice.

2 Cover and shake vigorously.

3 Strain into a chilled **COCKTAIL GLASS**, or into an ice-filled **ROCKS GLASS**.

★
FIVE POINTS
31 GREAT JONES STREET NYC 10012
www.fivepointsrestaurant.com
212-253-5700

INDIAN ROSE

TAJ

*I*NDIAN DRINKS ARE USUALLY LIMITED TO THAT SPICED TEA and milk concoction, chai. But at sexy Taj, where American dishes are reincarnated with Indian influences—such as Pan Roasted Lobster with "Biryani Rice," and "Tandoori" Red Snapper with Mushroom Ghee—even the house cocktails emphasize the flavors of the subcontinent. These drinks, conjured up by consulting mixologist Jerri Banks, dazzle with the flavors of masala tea and star anise, tamarind syrup and Earl Grey. There's even a creamy and cooling cocktail called the Manghi, made with Rhum Barbancourt, mango, and yogurt. However, the drink that best suits the sultry décor, with its imported Indian sandstone statues, teak screens, and booths piled with pillows, is the Indian Rose. The floral aromas of this drink are intoxicating without being overpowering, and they're carried aloft on the effervescence of Champagne. If you absolutely need that chai fix, I'd advise you take it in the form of a Chocolate Soufflé, complete with chocolate chai and raspberry sauces.

Normally, I don't think specific spirit brands are terribly important in creating a drink. As long as you use a good-quality spirit that you personally enjoy, you can usually tweak the balance and create an excellent cocktail. However, Hendrick's, a very soft Scottish gin, goes easy on the piney juniper flavors in favor of the essence of cucumber and rose petals, which proves critical for this drink. Rosebud Tea and rose syrup can be found in Indian and Middle Eastern specialty markets.

1½ ounces Hendrick's Gin
1 ounce Rosebud Tea
½ ounce rose syrup
½ ounce fresh lemon juice
2 ounces Moët et Chandon Champagne
Several unsprayed rose petals

1 Combine the gin, Rosebud Tea, rose syrup, and lemon juice in a cocktail shaker with ice.

2 Cover and shake vigorously.

3 Strain into a chilled **COCKTAIL GLASS.**

4 Top with Champagne and float a few rose petals on the surface.

PARIS, NEW JERSEY

NAKED LUNCH

WHEN YOU HAIL FROM NEW JERSEY, you learn at a young age that your home state is a favorite punching bag of New Yorkers. As a fellow New Jersey resident and bartender Gary Keating is my kindred soul. While I typically fight back using my pen, Keating uses his cocktail shaker. Taking his inspiration from the French Martini, he made some tweaks and dubbed it the Paris, New Jersey. "I originally created it in the Hamptons. I wanted to create something so good that people had to have it, but they absolutely have to order it by name or they don't get one," says Keating. And the best thing about Naked Lunch, besides the Latin dancing on Wednesday and the 1980s revival on the weekends, is that this hip SoHo spot welcomes all comers. You'll always find a bumpin' house of young professionals, Euro-tourists, other-borough folks, and yes, the cool people from New Jersey.

This cool purple drink is modeled on the French Martini, which traditionally consists only of vodka, pineapple juice, and Chambord. However, I make a different kind of "French" Martini by using Lillet Blanc in place of my usual dry vermouth. Perhaps "Bordeaux Martini" would be more descriptive of that drink, since the lovely white aperitif hails from the region.

2 ounces Grey Goose
1 ounce pineapple juice
1 ounce Chambord
Splash of sour mix
Splash of 7-Up

1 Combine the vodka, juice, Chambord, and sour mix in a cocktail shaker with ice.

2 Cover and shake vigorously.

3 Strain into a chilled COCKTAIL GLASS.

4 Finish with a splash of 7-Up.

'SANS'GRIA BLANCO

IXTA

THIS STYLISH RESTAURANT, named for Mexico's Iztaccihuatl mountain, takes artistic license with Mexican cuisine, offering dishes like Seared Tuna with Blood Orange Margarita Reduction and Roasted Chicken with Tamale Hash and Mole Reduction. And cocktail consultant Jerri Banks offers similarly inspired drinks, like her Sol Liso, a top-shelf margarita with mango puree. She also looks to Spain to hop on the citywide sangria revival with her 'Sans'gria Blanco, which forgoes the traditional red wine in favor of trendier white, as you might find in Barcelona. "As for the 'Sans'gria Blanco, the aromatics are not generally used in Mexico, but the finished product is a perfect foil for any cuisine. The cardamom's high-toned aroma bridges well to fragrant fare while the lemon thyme adds another layer of nuanced scent," says Banks. It really does go well with the savory Ixta cuisine, and like so many cocktails that succeed in this respect, it begins with wine.

Whether you're making your sangria with red wine or white, it's critical to allow the mixture to steep overnight to thoroughly extract the flavors of the fruit and allow the ingredients to mingle. In Spain there are many variations that use cava, brandy, and even cola in the mix.

1 gallon white wine, such as Pinot Grigio
1 cup fresh lemon juice
¼ cup cardamom pods, lightly crushed
8 to 10 sprigs lemon thyme
1 lemon sliced in ½-inch pieces
1 cup crushed green grapes
1 cup simple syrup
Sprig of lemon thyme
1 or 2 green grapes, sliced

1 Combine the first 7 ingredients in a nonreactive container. Refrigerate, and allow to steep for 24 hours.

2 Strain the wine into another container suitable for pouring.

3 Serve chilled over a small amount of ice in a WINE GLASS.

4 Garnish with sprig of thyme and sliced grapes.

MAKES ABOUT 18 SERVINGS

THE SHINING STAR

In 2002, The Ritz-Carlton made an encore appearance, following their new Battery Park property, by launching an equally lavish establishment in the former St. Moritz Hotel on Central Park South. In contrast to Chef Gabriel Kreuther's lauded restaurant, Atelier, The Ritz received little fanfare for its new cocktail lounge just outside the restaurant. But for barflies in the know, it meant the return of Norman. That's Norman Bukofzer, who by no coincidence manned the bar at the former Ritz-Carlton (now the Inter-Continental). His mere presence makes a drink a transporting experience at the stately bar, a quiet retreat from the swinging scene at Atelier. As he keeps the standing bar crowd entertained with barroom banter acquired over decades, Brooklyn-born Norman might be overheard doling out subway strategies or restaurant tips, but never celebrity gossip—though one can sense he's seen his share of shenanigans. Even when you're at The Ritz, it's really the bartender that makes the bar. And Norman is the consummate New York bartender.

At first glance, this drink is just a Cosmo with star fruit. Big deal, right? But actually, chilling the base spirit in the freezer first has a profound effect on a drink. By adding chilled Ketel One, the drink absorbs less water during shaking, resulting in a less diluted, rather potent drink.

2 ounces chilled Ketel One Citroen

¾ ounce Cointreau

Solid splash (slightly less than ½ ounce) of cranberry juice

½ ounce freshly squeezed lime juice

1 slice star fruit

1 Combine the vodka, Cointreau, cranberry juice, and lime juice in an ice-filled cocktail shaker.

2 Cover and shake vigorously.

3 Strain into a chilled **COCKTAIL GLASS.**

4 Garnish with the slice of star fruit.

Cocktail Chronicles
REST & RESTORATION

LUXURY HOTELS ARE AN INTEGRAL PART OF THE NEW YORK LANDSCAPE and social scene, and their reputations are often shaped by their bars and lounges. For more than a century, hotel bars have been a place where business deals were sealed, celebrities were sighted, and expert bartenders practiced their craft. When the city's hotels first began to emulate their high-amenity European counterparts in the late 1800s, the bar was often a primary source of steady income—the bar customers more reliable than the stream of visitors that came to stay. While independent bars found staying power by serving plentiful,

cheap ale, it was in the gilded bars of hotels that the cocktail culture of the city was born. Like the private clubs that were popular in the late nineteenth century, hotel bars were originally open to men only. Bartenders remained with a single hotel for years and developed a close following of patrons. But when Prohibition came, hotel bars were, unlike taverns, highly visible and thus unable to convert to speakeasies. Most hotel

bars were out of service during the twenties. The Waldorf-Astoria's famous bar was forced to close, and soon after the entire hotel was out of business. The grand Hoffman House Hotel with its ornate bar (above, 1898) also had to shut its doors. Others, such as the Plaza's Oak Bar (page 32), were able to reopen and regain their place as important social and business arenas after Prohibition's repeal. Today, though cocktails are served on almost every block of the city, hotel bars offer a quieter and more traditional bar experience. At bars like Bemelmans at the Carlyle (page 96) and the Star Lounge at The Ritz-Carlton Central Park South, one can find a swank setting, impeccable service, and a respite from harried city life.

PRICKLY PEAR MARGARITA

WITH ALL OF THE HEAT AND SPICE ON THE PLATES, it's fitting that the best margaritas here are frozen. But that was an easy conclusion for Eben Klemm, director of cocktails for all of owner Stephen Hanson's B. R. Guest restaurants around town. What distinguishes Dos Caminos from the rest of the pack is the bar atmosphere, which seems to be far more fun than the dining room. Given the range of playful cocktails Klemm has conjured up here, it's easy to see why. Even the ubiquitous Cosmopolitan is given a jolt by way of the Cosmo del Diablo, which combines chile-infused vodka, passion fruit juice, and pineapple juice, making for a spicy-sweet concoction that's strangely irresistible. Purists will enjoy sipping their way through the commendable collection of 150 tequilas. But the real reason to come here is for the famous Prickly Pear Margarita.

CACTUS PEAR PUREE

1 Wash and peel ripe prickly pears.
2 Cut in half with a knife and discard the seeds.
3 Force the raw pulp through a medium-to-fine strainer.
4 Freeze puree until needed.

1½ ounces tequila
½ ounce triple sec or Citrónge Liqueur
1 ounce fresh lime juice
Dash of cactus pear puree
1 lime wheel

1 Pour the tequila, triple sec, lime juice, and cactus pear puree into an ice-filled blender.

2 Blend until smooth.

3 Pour into a short-stemmed **PARFAIT GLASS** and garnish with the lime wheel.

You can find fresh cactus pears practically year-round at gourmet produce stands and markets to make this puree, which can be frozen in batches. You could also buy it prepared at better markets, too.

Chapter 5

CREATIVE LICENSE

HARLEM NIGHTS

SUFFERING BASTARD

SPRING FLING

LIBERTINI

RUSSIAN RUBLE

BLUE MÉTRAZUR

MAMBO KING

MOROCCAN MARTINI

KENTUCKY PEAR

THE VOLCANO

SPIKED LEMONADE

FROZEN PINEAPPLE MARGARITA

VALENTINO

TROTSKY

MATILDA

LOVE

WET WATER MARTINI

BASIL-MINT MOJITO

LEMONADE COOLER

NORTHERN SEX ON THE BEACH

HARLEM NIGHTS

THE LENOX LOUNGE

THE REBIRTH AND RESTORATION of Harlem's legendary Lenox Lounge is nothing short of a miracle, given all the curveballs fate has thrown its way. Since it opened in 1939 it has hosted some of the jazz and blues world's greatest names, including Billie Holliday, John Coltrane, and Miles Davis, but fell on some pretty hard times before the current cocktail—and Harlem—renaissance. The Art Deco interior has been lovingly refurbished, the beautiful tiled floors and mirrors restored, including the fin-bladed light towers. The Zebra Room, with its famous banquettes, is perfect for twosomes here to take in a local act or groove to the DJ. At the well-worn bar you should order the smooth, smoky Harlem Nights, which sounds sweeter on paper than it tastes. In fact, the coffee liqueur adds a note of bittersweet—perfectly appropriate in this space.

Although this drink doesn't name specific booze brands, here are two suggestions if you're wondering what to buy. For coconut-flavored rum, consider Malibu; and for coffee liqueur try Kahlúa.

3 ounces tequila

3 ounces coconut-flavored rum

2 ounces coffee liqueur

Splash of pineapple juice

Splash of peach schnapps

1 maraschino cherry

1 orange wheel

1 In a cocktail shaker, combine the tequila, rum, coffee liqueur, and pineapple juice.

2 Top with ice, cover, and shake vigorously.

3 Strain into an ice-filled **COLLINS GLASS**.

4 Top with peach schnapps and garnish with the cherry and the orange wheel.

SUFFERING BASTARD

*C*IBAR MAY AS WELL BE A SPEAKEASY, given its covert location in the basement of The Inn at Irving Place. The Inn itself, two conjoined Wharton-era brownstones, displays no name, either, making the whole shebang an insider's venue from the outset. The bar is a small, cozy, old-fashioned affair, where quiet conversation in one of the loveseats by the open fire is about as loud as it gets. In fact, the oohs and aahs you'll hear below the guestrooms come from the bar itself, where general manager Gina Pepperdine mixes up her flaming "Suffering Bastard," a drink that seems as out of place here as a Mai Tai. Pepperdine took the drink's inspiration from years working at resorts where Polynesian drinks ruled, one of which inspired this creation. The one made here, however, has no umbrella or pineapple totem pole, but rather is served in a cocktail glass with a flaming lemon floater. The flaming part might seem a little kitschy, but the drink itself is a lovely assemblage of a trio of rums balanced with as many fruit juices. It's both fun to make and quite easy to drink.

1 ounce Captain Morgan Original
　　Spiced Rum
¾ ounce Malibu Rum
¾ ounce Myers's Original Dark Rum
1 ounce fresh pineapple juice
1 ounce fresh orange juice
1 ounce cranberry juice
1 lemon heel (see Tip)
½ ounce high-proof rum

1 In an ice-filled cocktail shaker combine the first three rums and the three juices.

2 Cover and shake thoroughly.

3 Fill the lemon heel with the high-proof rum and set it in a **COCKTAIL GLASS** on the table where the drink is to be served. Light rum carefully with a match.

4 Slowly strain the cocktail into the glass, running it carefully down the side from the lip (this will cause the flaming lemon shell to rise to the top).

5 When your guest is duly impressed, carefully pour the remaining cocktail mixture on top of the flame to extinguish it.

This cocktail calls for a high-proof rum that will ignite easily and burn off quickly, such as Bacardi 151. Of course, you could just as easily use one of the rums used to mix this drink. Whatever the medium just be very careful. To create lemon heel, cut off the bottom third of a whole lemon and scoop out the flesh from the heel, being careful to keep the rind intact. Now you have a lemon heel that will serve as a tiny cup, a cocktail within your cocktail.

SPRING FLING

*T*HE DOUBLE ENTENDRE THIS COCKTAIL'S MONIKER implies is well-suited to this very intimate, cozy bar within the boutique hotel The Mark. I can't get a bartender to dish on a single tryst he's witnessed, but I've been assured with a wink that the drink's name was chosen for its allusion to the lightness of spring and what a few of these concoctions may lead to in these close quarters. Ironically, I can think of no better room in which to spend a cold winter evening than this opulent living room-of-a-bar, replete with plush chairs, dark mahogany wood, and thick carpeting. They even serve light fare from the adjoining Mark's Restaurant. The service in both rooms is first class, and judging by the tight lips of the bartender, if you're here for more than a Spring Fling cocktail, your secret is in very good hands.

Bar manager John Cardarelli is a passionate perfectionist when it comes to cocktails, and one imperfection he sees often when watching others prepare them is that they don't have glassware ready for the incoming drink. "I cannot stress the importance of preparing a presentation glass before you begin making a cocktail." If you're not prepared, the cocktail sits in the shaker too long and starts to get watered down.

2 ounces silver tequila
½ ounce triple sec
1 ounce fresh orange juice
1 ounce fresh pineapple juice
1 lime wheel

1 Into an ice-filled cocktail shaker pour the tequila, triple sec, and juices.

2 Cover and shake thoroughly.

3 Strain into a **ROCKS GLASS** filled with crushed ice, or into a chilled **COCKTAIL GLASS**.

4 Garnish with the lime wheel.

LIBERTINI

HERE ARE MORE PARKS THAN BARS WORTH VISITING in this hood, but those of us who don't own rollerblades can stake out our own vista on the fourteenth floor of the Ritz-Carlton's Downtown outpost. At Rise, the magnificent views of New York Harbor, Ellis Island, and, of course, the Statue of Liberty, are the best you find without boarding the Circle Line. I suggest sitting on the terrace when the weather permits, firing up one of the restaurant's hibachis, and grilling your own Harissa Rubbed Lamb or Cilantro Marinated Shrimp. The twenty-five-ounce Tumbler drinks, like Sangria D'Cava, are intended to be shared by three or four. (Nobody told me, all right?) Rise has even concocted the ideal drink to raise a glass to Lady Liberty, the Libertini—a drink that, incidentally, joins a very short list of green drinks that will ever pass my lips. After that Tumbler and a Libertini I could almost see the statue toasting me with a drink in her hand.

2 ounces citrus-flavored vodka
½ ounce pear liqueur
½ ounce Midori Melon
¼ ounce blue curaçao
Splash of fresh lemon juice
1 orange twist

1 In an ice-filled cocktail shaker combine the vodka, liqueurs, and juice.

2 Cover and shake thoroughly.

3 Strain into a chilled COCKTAIL GLASS.

4 Garnish with orange twist.

West Street forms the eastern boundary of Battery Park City, a 92-acre community owned and operated by the Battery Park City Authority. The land for the project was reclaimed from the Hudson River by filling in old piers with construction excavation, much of which came from the World Trade Center; the terra firma itself was only completed in 1976.

The melon liqueur Midori was first released in the United States in 1978 at a party at the hottest nightclub of the time, Studio 54. Known for its celebrity clientele and abundant drugs, Studio 54 came to epitomize the indulgence and excesses of the New York club scene of that era. The club shut down for good in 1986, but Midori fared much better. It continues to be a popular mixer, especially in bartending competitions, and it helps give the Libertini its color. As one of the first fruit-based liqueurs, it led the way for today's variety of flavored vodkas and rums.

RUSSIAN RUBLE

FIREBIRD

MY FAVORITE DRINK AT FIREBIRD is the house specialty, Honey Vodka, but the recipe is a guarded secret going back at least three generations, according to everyone I tried to bribe there. All I could muster from the bar manager is that its foundation is Luksusowa Potato Vodka from Poland and that twenty different herbs and spices are added before it's sent to the pastry kitchen to be "laced with honey." They serve 500 glasses of the stuff a day, and it's absolutely ethereal with blini and caviar. Alas, you'll have to go there to taste it. At home, however, you could easily replicate my second favorite drink there, the Russian Ruble, a hilariously downscale name for a drink served in a double townhouse decorated to represent the height of Russian aristocracy, circa 1912. That means the ceiling is painted gold, the bar is marble, and the service is exemplary, with waiters sporting uniforms purportedly designed by Oleg Cassini. Naturally, the Russian Ruble has a fittingly regal red glow by way of cranberry juice, which gives the drink tart refreshment.

If you're intrigued by FireBird's secret Honey Vodka recipe, you should feel free to experiment with trying to make some at home. The beauty of vodka in general is that it takes on whatever flavor it's introduced to, so if you steep it with fresh fruit, for example, or dried spices, you'll undoubtedly taste them in the vodka long after you strain them out. In the case of FireBird's Honey Vodka, the honey is apparently added just before it's served. If anyone figures out this recipe, please send it to me.

1 ounce vodka
½ ounce Malibu Rum
½ ounce Cuervo Gold
2 ounces cranberry juice
1 lemon twist

1 In an ice-filled cocktail shaker, combine the vodka, rum, tequila, and juice.

2 Cover and shake thoroughly.

3 Strain into an ice-filled ROCKS GLASS. Garnish with the lemon twist.

BLUE MÉTRAZUR

MÉTRAZUR

*A*S IF THERE WEREN'T ALREADY ENOUGH REASONS for a noncommuter to visit Grand Central Terminal, Métrazur, Charlie Palmer's sleek American brasserie, is yet another, with the hook being the unparalleled view across the entire concourse from this very public bar way up on the East Balcony. Surprisingly, the few times I've enjoyed a drink here the bar wasn't too crowded—although, given the scale of the surroundings, it might have been an optical illusion. Regardless, the barstools are high enough so that you can see over the marble balustrade, as well as get a great view of the giant mirror overhead, making this a prime locale for people watching—or stargazing at the magnificent ceiling. And of course for enjoying a cocktail such as the Blue Métrazur, a citrusy concoction spiked with brandy, that was crafted to put us in a Mediterranean mindset, which is apropos, after all, since the restaurant is named for a train that once ran along the Côte d'Azur en route to Monaco. Alas, there's no casino here.

2 ounces Absolut Citron
¼ ounce apricot brandy
Splash of blue curaçao
Splash of lemon juice

1 In a cocktail shaker, combine all ingredients.

2 Fill the glass with ice, cover, and shake thoroughly.

3 Strain into a chilled **COCKTAIL GLASS**.

This drink gets its color from a liqueur called blue curaçao, which is, yes, a blue-tinted curaçao—but what exactly is curaçao? It's basically a general term for an orange-flavored liqueur made from the peel of bitter oranges grown on the Caribbean island of Curaçao. It always starts out as a clear spirit to which color is added—there's orange, blue, green, and, when left clear, "white." Regardless of its color, it still tastes like sweetened bitter oranges.

MAMBO KING

ASIA DE CUBA

*H*IPSTERS STILL FLOCK TO RUB ELBOWS at this Asian–Latin fusion restaurant in Ian Schrager's Morgans Hotel—quite literally, in fact, since this is where anointed designer Philippe Starck introduced New Yorkers to the communal dining table, with a marble monolith that seats thirty-six. Starck has cast the dining room in suitably flattering light and draped it with white curtains, making everyone appear backlit. And the high design extends to the cocktails, as well. Take the Mambo King, sort of a Kir Royale with a kick, courtesy of raspberry-flavored vodka. The drink, like the room, suggests neither Asia nor Cuba. The food, however, excites the palate with fiery Latin flavors fused with the clean purity of Asian ingredients. Being a consummate carnivore, I adore the Rum Roast Pork, but the Tunapica—raw tuna blended with olives, almonds, and black currant—is not to be missed.

Grenadine syrup
Raw sugar
2 ounces raspberry-flavored vodka
8 ounces Champagne, well-chilled

1 Dip the rim of a chilled
  CHAMPAGNE FLUTE into a saucer
  of grenadine followed by the sugar
  "in the raw."

2 Pour in the raspberry vodka and
  top with the Champagne.

The history of Champagne—both the drink and the region—is long and celebrated. Names like Dom Perignon and Möet et Chandon add to the sparkling wine's reputation of elegance, so it may seem like sacrilege to drink champagne in anything but a pure, unmixed form. But Champagne can add the perfect kick to a cocktail. To make a Champagne Cocktail, use 6 ounces to cover a cube of sugar and 2 dashes of Angostura bitters in a Champagne flute. You can top it off with an ounce of cognac, or simply garnish with a lemon twist.

MOROCCAN MARTINI

*T*HIS ENDURING LEGEND OF A BAR has transitioned from hotspot in the 1980s into an institution in the 1990s and reached icon status today in the new century. With its retro burgundy and black banquettes, beautiful Deco bar, and lazy ceiling fans, The Odeon feels comfortable and unpretentious pretty much any time of day or night. And the classic brasserie menu hardly changes, so you always feel like an insider here—even if it's been a few years since your last visit. In other words, The Odeon is a comfortable oasis, or at least that's the connection I make as I sit down to sip bartender Abdul Tabini's Moroccan Martini. Tabini, who hails from Casablanca, crafted the cocktail with the heat of his homeland and the pleasure of refreshment, making a simple drink that's not at all sweet, in fact slightly tart, and rendered mouthwatering by fresh mint—an oasis in the desert.

5 fresh mint leaves
¼ teaspoon sugar
3 ounces Stoli Ohranj
1 teaspoon fresh lime juice
Splash of simple syrup

1 In a cocktail shaker, muddle 4 of the mint leaves with the sugar.

2 Add ice, vodka, lime juice, and simple syrup.

3 Cover and shake thoroughly.

4 Strain into a chilled COCKTAIL GLASS.

5 Garnish with remaining mint leaf, floating on top.

Sweet is one of the primary tastes used to balance cocktails; it comes in many forms. Sugar, for instance, is most convenient when dissolved in simple syrup. But certain cocktails require granules for muddling or for adding texture to the final drink. In addition to standard granulated sugar, a well-equipped bar will also have powdered (confectioners') sugar and quick-dissolving (superfine) sugar.

KENTUCKY PEAR

*D*ON'T LET THE GIANT PUCCI LAMPS and sleek teak here fool you: This isn't a power lunch yawner, despite the Midtown address. Beacon's success is solidly grounded in both the kitchen and the bar, specifically because the cocktails reach far beyond the Cosmo klatch. The connection between my favorite drink here and Chef Waldy Malouf's menu is wood. Let me explain. The predominant spirit in the Kentucky Pear is Jim Beam Black bourbon, an 86-proof powerhouse that's aged eight years in charred white oak barrels, rendering it pleasantly smoky, slightly sweet, and very smooth. What does that have to do with the menu? Everything here is cooked over an open fire: Charred Filet Mignon Tartare, Wood Roasted Catskill Mountain Trout, and Spit Roasted Ten Herb Chicken, to name a few. But the real draw is the exceptional cocktail list at the tiny bar whence, I'd safely bet, they ring up as much in sales as they do at the tables. Now you know.

1½ ounces Jim Beam Black
¼ ounce Poire William eau de vie
¾ ounce simple syrup
¾ ounce fresh lemon juice
Splash of cranberry juice
1 pear slice (optional)

1 In an ice-filled cocktail shaker, combine the bourbon, eau de vie, syrup, and juices.

2 Cover and shake vigorously.

3 Strain into an ice-filled ROCKS GLASS.

4 Garnish with a pear slice, if you like.

With all this talk about charred wood and open fires, it would seem mandatory that you taste the Jim Beam Black bourbon by itself before you blend it into a cocktail. I believe you'll be pleasantly surprised by its subtle power, balanced by those telltale flavors of smoke and sweet caramel. Now you're ready for a cocktail.

Poire William eau de vie is a generic spirit term, rather than a specific brand, and it refers to a clear brandy distilled from pears. Traditionally it hails from the Alsace region of France and from Switzerland, and takes its name from a French pear variety called Williams Bon-Chrétien, which we know as the Bartlett. Amazingly, some bottles have a whole pear floating inside, a maddening task accomplished by placing a bottle over the just-budding fruit and forcing the pear to grow inside—while dangling from the tree. Naturally, you should expect to pay more for such bottlings.

THE VOLCANO

THE COCKTAIL ROOM

*I*N A NEIGHBORHOOD OVERFLOWING WITH IRISH-THEMED BEER bars, the Cocktail Room seems totally out of place because it's so, well, tastefully done. The décor is retro-chic without being cheeky, possessing a quasi-European flair that perhaps reflects the sensibilities of cofounder Stanley Bressler, a Ukrainian immigrant who learned the ins and outs of this city as a cabbie for twenty-two years before opening this swanky soiree room with his stepson Izzy Gotto in 2000. The cocktails run the gamut from classics to way-out-there concoctions—like the Banana Monkey, a frappe made with Bacardi Light, crème de banana, cream, and a splash of grenadine—the likes of which I'm sure Mr. Bressler described to Mr. Gotto as being all the rage when he arrived in New York from Odessa in the mid-1970s. One holdover from that era that I think is perfect for a date is a drink that must be shared, such as The Volcano, a monster of a drink, flaming presentation and all, that doesn't register as a serious classic by any means, but rather as an inspired infusion that suggests clever playfulness as well as daring intimacy. In other words, a perfect date.

The Cocktail Room's Volcano Bowl is served in their signature volcano-shaped bowl, which you will not likely find in your cupboard. However, you could use a small, stainless steel mixing bowl, or an ovenproof ceramic bowl. Of course, if you're making this for yourself and a friend with whom you'd prefer not to share (but really, what's the point?), strain the drink into two Collins glasses filled with crushed ice and mixed fruit—but forget about the flaming unless you're sure the glass can handle the heat.

2½ ounces Captain Morgan Original Spiced Rum
2½ ounces vodka
½ ounce pineapple juice
½ ounce cranberry juice
Assorted fruits, in chunks (pineapples, apples, oranges, berries)
High-proof rum for flaming
Straws for sharing

1 In an ice-filled cocktail shaker, combine the spiced rum, vodka, and juices.

2 Cover and shake vigorously.

3 Strain into a large, crushed-ice-filled, flameproof vessel.

4 Stir in assorted fruits.

5 Drizzle the high-proof rum on top and light when serving.

6 Serve with the straws on the side.

SPIKED LEMONADE

GOTHAM BAR AND GRILL

I CLEARLY REMEMBER THE FIRST TIME I stayed a little too long at the bar at Gotham Bar and Grill—I was probably as old as this restaurant is now—and decided I should have something to eat if I wanted to continue imbibing. I'd eaten at bars before, of course, but no one had ever snapped open a white linen napkin and placed it down before me to make a private table-cloth-for-one as the bartender did that night. I wound up staying until closing in my well-appointed perch near the wall, taking in the whole scene from the best seat in the house. Although that was two decades ago, I nearly repeated that tradition one hot afternoon when a friend and I stopped in for chef/owner Alfred Portale's Spiked Lemonade. We intended to have just one, but since it's made by the pitcher, well, we couldn't let it go to waste. And late afternoon became early evening.

Juice of 18 lemons

½ cup sugar

½ cup water

1 lemon, thinly sliced into wheels

Leaves from 2 sprigs of mint (optional)

12 ounces (1½ cups) raspberry-flavored vodka or homemade raspberry vodka

1 In a large pitcher, stir together the lemon juice and sugar until the sugar dissolves.

2 Add the water, stir, and taste. Add more sugar if necessary for sweetness, but keep in mind that when served the ice will dilute the lemonade a little.

3 Fill another pitcher or individual COLLINS GLASSES with ice.

4 Add the lemon slices and mint leaves, if using them, to the pitcher or glasses.

5 Mix the vodka into the lemonade and pour it over the ice.

6 Stir and serve.

MAKES ABOUT 1½ QUARTS, 8 SERVINGS

Superchef Alfred Portale, who likes to cook up cocktails in addition to his primary role here, naturally prefers to make his own raspberry-infused vodka. He simply steeps raspberries in a bottle of vodka—Level is his preference—and then freezes it. "This makes for a smooth, flavorful homemade vodka," he attests, and says the lemonade can be spiked with other flavored vodkas, too, such as mandarin, lemon, or orange. Hey chef, how about pink lemonade? "Just add a splash of cassis." Of course.

FROZEN PINEAPPLE MARGARITA

NOCHE

I HAPPEN TO HAVE A VERY PERSONAL RELATIONSHIP WITH FROZEN MARGARITAS because I actually made them—hundreds of thousands of them—when I tended bar at what was once one of the most popular bars in Hoboken, New Jersey, called East LA—a restaurant known more for its kick-ass margaritas than its Tex-Mex food. I should add that these were no ordinary margaritas: They were so strong that the management imposed a limit of three per person, primarily because the fruit flavoring in the already heady concoctions came by way of liqueurs, spiking them even higher in potency. All of this has nothing to do with Noche's Frozen Pineapple Margaritas, but because I typically eschew frozen cocktails, this one merits mentioning because it perfectly fits this steamy, Latin locale, and is delicious because it employs real pineapple. While Noche's downstairs bar is certainly lively, I prefer the throbbing chaos upstairs in the multilevel lounge with its retro white leather banquettes. Noche might be in the middle of Times Square, but it sure feels like south of the border here.

Granulated sugar
Pineapple wedge for garnish
2 ounces pineapple-infused tequila
1 ounce triple sec
2 ounces fresh lime juice
1 ounce simple syrup

1 Fill a saucer with enough sugar to coat the rim of a glass.

2 Rub the rim of a **PARFAIT GLASS** or a **COLLINS GLASS** with the pineapple, then dip the rim into the sugar to coat thoroughly.

3 Fill a blender halfway with ice. Add the tequila, triple sec, lime juice, and simple syrup.

4 Cover and blend until homogeneous and thick.

5 Pour into the sugared glass and garnish with the pineapple.

Noche's Frozen Pineapple Margarita calls for pineapple-infused tequila, which you probably won't find in a liquor store. Unlike flavored vodkas, tequilas are almost never sold preflavored, probably because they already possess so many wonderful, complex nuances. (Infusing vodkas was all the rage at many bars in the early 1990s, until flavored vodkas took hold.) For this drink, you could either create your own infusion, by steeping pineapple chunks in tequila for as long as it takes to impart significant flavor—anywhere from a few hours to two weeks—or you could cheat by pureeing pineapples, straining them through a sieve or cheesecloth, and using that pure extract to flavor your tequila. Or you could just go to Noche and let them do it for you.

VALENTINO

*A*LPHABET CITY HAS GONE FROM BLEAK TO CHIC over the past decade, and this sexy neighborhood bistro, helmed by owner and executive chef Alex Freij, caters to the new—and less grungy—denizens of the East Village, beautiful as they are. The name issues a not-so-subtle reminder that the place is about food, and the Lobster Bruschetta alone, heaped with succulent white meat, is worth the price of admission. Yummy reminders of Freij's French mentors, Jean-Louis Palladin and Jean-Georges Vongerichten, include a crunchy Duck Confit. But it's the atmosphere at Industry that truly dazzles. The place is ensconced in shiny wood, and includes cozy, dark banquettes swathed in candlelight, along with birch trees that soar to the top of the atrium and sway to the beat of the downstairs lounge DJ—sort of Swiss Family Robinson meets Sly and the Family Stone. And of course, it all works magnificently.

Grenadine, which has graced the Shirley Temple for decades, is, in theory, sweetened pomegranate syrup. In reality, most bottled grenadine is nothing more than red sugar water. To add a dose of authenticity, you can make your own grenadine. Combine about a cup of pomegranate juice (available in health food stores and some supermarkets) with an equal amount of water and about half as much sugar in a saucepan. Reduce over low heat until you achieve a syrupy consistency.

1 ounce passion fruit puree
¾ ounce Stolichnaya Strasberi
Splash of simple syrup
Splash of fresh lime juice
Splash of grenadine
4 ounces Champagne
1 whole strawberry

1 In an ice-filled cocktail shaker, combine the puree, vodka, syrup, juice, and grenadine.

2 Cover and shake thoroughly.

3 Strain into a **CHAMPAGNE FLUTE.**

4 Top with the Champagne.

5 Garnish with the strawberry.

With the arrival of Industry and other top-notch watering holes, this 'hood hardly resembles early-1990s Alphabet City. But the zeitgeist of this era is preserved in our cultural conscience thanks to the international success of Jonathan Larson's Rent, a tale of local artists set here and loosely based on La Bohème. Rent still resonates with audiences today.

THE TROTSKY

*A*T FIRST GLANCE, "KGB BAR" might appear to be just another kitschy name. But in reality, it pays homage to the former occupants of this second-floor bar, a local band of the Ukrainian socialists. Furthermore, KGB proudly preserves the spirit of revolution with a tightly knit group of literati comrades who come to read their work among the Constructivist propaganda posters, with separate evenings dedicated to fiction, non-fiction, and poetry. In the true spirit of socialism: No one gets paid. No one pays. Drinking, however, is encouraged. Vodka, beer, maybe a shot of Jack, seem to be the drinks of choice. But The Trotsky cocktail pays tribute to one man's mighty pen. Oddly, it's made with tequila, not vodka—perhaps as a tribute to Leon Trotsky's admission to Mexico in 1937 at the behest of artists Diego Rivera and Frida Kahlo.

3 ounces tequila
Dash of triple sec
Dash of Rose's sweetened lime juice
1 ounce cranberry juice or 1 splash of grenadine

1 In an ice-filled cocktail shaker, combine all ingredients.

2 Cover and shake thoroughly.

3 Strain into a chilled **COCKTAIL GLASS.**

The Trotsky calls specifically for Rose's sweetened lime juice, a mixer with a long history and many uses. In the nineteenth century, Lauchlin Rose, a Scottish shipbuilder, patented a lime and rum mixture to prevent scurvy in soldiers who traveled long months between ports. British sailors then became known as "limeys." It later appeared in drinks such as the Gimlet, named, appropriately, after a medical officer in the British Royal Navy. The Gimlet is made up of 2 ounces of gin and 2 ounces of Rose's lime juice. Stir these together in an ice-filled shaker, strain into a cocktail glass, and garnish with a lime wedge.

New Yorkers came very close to inheriting some of Mexican muralist Diego Rivera's public work. Nelson Rockefeller persuaded Rivera to create a mural for the newly built Rockefeller Center in 1933. However, when the face of Lenin made a surprise appearance in the painting, New York's greatest capitalist was not amused. The two failed to reach an agreement. Rivera was ordered to stop and the painting was removed. Rivera later went on to paint Portrait of America for the New Workers School in New York City, including great Americans like Ben Franklin, Thomas Paine, and Walt Whitman in the murals.

MATILDA

WHILE THIS HISTORIC HOTEL lends its name to the Algonquin cocktail—comprised of whiskey, French vermouth, and pineapple juice—the cocktail is not one of my true favorites. And history suggests that the literati of the famous Round Table—including Dorothy Parker, Robert Benchley, and Harold Ross, creator of *The New Yorker*—were more partial to martinis as dry as their wit, anyway. The Blue Bar is more casual than the famous Oak Room (which still requires a jacket), making it perfect for a pre-theater pop-in for some tasty pub fare or my favorite house tipple: the Matilda. Named after the house cat who commands the lobby, the drink makes a suitable nod to the Champagne cocktails of the past and, like Parker herself, balances a mellifluous entry with just enough bite.

When mixing any drink with Champagne, club soda, or other sparkling beverage, never add the carbonated liquid to the shaker, or you will lose the fizz and possibly create a disaster. These ingredients are always added, pre-chilled, to the final mixed drink.

1½ ounces Absolut Mandrin
½ ounce Cointreau
Juice of 1 orange
1 ounce Moët et Chandon Champagne
1 orange twist

1 Combine the vodka, Cointreau, and juice in a cocktail shaker with ice.

2 Cover and shake vigorously.

3 Strain into a chilled COCKTAIL GLASS.

4 Top with the Champagne.

5 Garnish with the twist of orange.

THE MUSE OF BOOZE

FOR WRITERS IN THE CITY, New York's bars have always been a place to gather, argue, and even compose their next work. In particular, Greenwich Village has long been a nexus for writers and artists, from Walt Whitman in the nineteenth century to the Beats in the twentieth. Some landmark bars still stand in the neighborhood, including the White Horse Tavern, where the poet Dylan Thomas literally drank himself to death in 1938. Later, the founders of the Village Voice—Norman Mailer, Dan Wolf, and Ed Fancher—met weekly at the White Horse. Jack Kerouac, a familiar face in many of New York's bars in his day, visited the tavern with such frequency that he once found "Kerouac go home!" written on the men's room wall. Nearby, Chumley's (below) preserved its Prohibition-era feel while serving as a favorite watering hole for the likes of J. D. Salinger, John Cheever, Upton Sinclair, Sinclair Lewis, and many more. The book jackets of its many literary customers still grace the walls of Chumley's today. Another literary landmark that hasn't changed is the infamous McSorely's, a tavern where only one drink—beer—is served, and which the poet E. E. Cummings called "snug and evil." A bit brighter and more spacious, Pete's Tavern (page 150), where O. Henry wrote his famous story "The Gift of the Magi," remains open today. Uptown, the more refined Algonquin Hotel bar was the gathering place in the 1920s for the Round Table group of writers, which included Dorothy Parker, Robert Benchley, and Harold Ross, who founded The New Yorker with money provided by the hotel.

LOVE

*D*URING THE LATE NINETEENTH CENTURY, Rockefellers, Vanderbilts, and Roosevelts led the charge to create the great camps in the Adirondacks in upstate New York. Their summertime exodus to the virgin lakelands marked a return to nature and created a whole new style of luxurious, yet rustic, life. And with Merc Bar, restaurateur and publisher John McDonald has once again lured the elite with warm-hued wood and antlers, canoes and copper—only this time the retreat is much closer to home. So close, in fact, that you can watch the city buzzing by through large windows even while reclining in the idyllic environs. With its exposed brick and rugged interior, the Merc inspired countless imitators, but this original has actually transcended trendy and become more of a cozy neighborhood hangout. The Love cocktail is really a top-shelf Margarita with a hint of raspberry. It's aptly named, because at this romantic lodge, love is the only thing people are actually hunting.

2½ ounces Sauza Tequila Conmemorativo

½ ounce Cointreau

½ ounce Chambord

½ ounce sour mix

1/2 ounce fresh lime juice

2 ounces fresh orange juice

1 lime wheel

1 Combine the tequila, Cointreau, Chambord, sour mix, and juices in a cocktail shaker with ice.

2 Cover and shake vigorously.

3 Strain into a chilled COCKTAIL GLASS.

4 Garnish with the lime wheel.

Sauza Tequila Conmemorativo is a blue agave tequila aged in bourbon casks for up to four years to give it an oaky, smooth finish.

WET WATER MARTINI

CCORDING TO COLOR PSYCHOLOGISTS, it's the red walls, red carpet, red lighting, and red pool table that are causing my heart to flutter, my blood pressure to rise, and my libido to ignite. Of course, the striking brunette delivering my Wet Water Martini, then pausing to reapply lip gloss, has nothing to do with it, right? Cherry caters to the same cute clientele usually drawn to nightlife mogul Randy Gerber's more famous Whiskey Bar, and here Gerber and the W New York–The Tuscany have clearly turned up the innuendo. My drink is wet, yes, but I'm relieved it's not red and has no cherry in it. The overhead mirror offers a parting glimpse of my lacquered-lips waitress, as well as attractive couples feeding each other small bites and inching closer on the (yes, red) leather banquettes. I can only imagine how they might be entwined by the 4:00 am closing.

Don't even think of using another gin for this cocktail. Beefeater Wet is a totally unique product with a final flavoring of natural pear that greatly enhances the drink.

2 ounces Beefeater Wet Gin

½ ounce Chambord

1½ ounce Power-C Vitamin Water

1 pear slice

1 Combine gin, Chambord, and vitamin water in an ice-filled cocktail shaker.

2 Cover and shake vigorously.

3 Strain into a chilled COCKTAIL GLASS.

4 Garnish with the pear slice.

BASIL-MINT MOJITO

*T*HIS NEXT-DOOR ANNEX OF TOM COLICCHIO'S build-your-own-meal restaurant Craft offers a substantial menu, and, more importantly, twice the number of house cocktails as its namesake. Among the six seasonal drinks, none misses its mark. The Craftbar Cocktail is a basic Bellini made with fresh fruit in season. The Ginger Martini warms the palate without searing, and a Blackberry Margarita lets the unctuous agave of El Tesoro Tequila burst through. But my favorite is the Basil-Mint Mojito, mixed sufficiently tart, made with Pyrat rum and chopped basil that adds a welcome top note of licorice. Rows of two-tops in the narrow dining room and an open kitchen make this a great date destination, but service for one at the bar also deserves praise. Many of the appetizers make perfect cocktail fare, from the Wild Boar Stuffed Sage Leaves to a warm dish of chewy pecorino, topped with the sweet heat of acacia honey and pepperoncini with crunchy hazelnuts.

Ernest Hemingway is almost as famous for his drinking habits as his prose, and he developed both in the years he spent in Cuba. He once wrote on a napkin, "I have my daiquiris at Floridita, and my mojitos at Bodeguita." The daiquiri—made by shaking 1 ½ ounces of light rum, the juice of half a lime, and one teaspoon of sugar in an ice-filled shaker—is traditionally served, strained, in a cocktail glass. Today the frozen daiquiri is much more popular, but the original is still served at the Bodeguita in Havana, where Hemingway's quote, among other memorabilia, is posted on the walls.

3 mint leaves
3 basil leaves
1 ounce fresh lime juice
2 ounces white Pyrat Rum
1 ounce simple syrup
Spash of club soda
1 lime wedge

1 Tear the mint and basil leaves into small pieces and place them in a **COLLINS GLASS** with the lime juice, rum, and simple syrup.

2 Muddle the leaves and the liquid.

3 Fill the glass with ice and top off with club soda.

4 Garnish with the lime wedge.

craftbar

LEMONADE COOLER

*T*HIS GRAMERCY ANTIQUITY WAS ESTABLISHED IN 1864, and hasn't stopped slinging beers since. They actually operated through Prohibition disguised as a flower shop, under the protection of nearby Tammany Hall politicos—not that it was ever tough to find a drink in New York during those thirteen most embarrassing years of United States history. This achievement has earned Pete's recognition as an official historical landmark, the oldest continuously operating bar in the city. Most impressively, the place is relatively unchanged, right down to the 30-foot rosewood bar, making this a real bar-lover's bar. You're likely to recognize Pete's from cameos on New York-centric hits such as *Seinfeld*, *Law and Order*, and *Sex and the City*, as well as a few major motion pictures and a bunch of beer commercials. And while many of the regulars go for a brew and a sampling of the reasonably priced Italian-American standards, like parmigiana and scaloppine of everything, the Lemonade Cooler is definitely aimed at the ladies, who for many years were absolutely not welcome here.

½ ounce Grand Marnier
½ ounce Chambord
5 ounces fresh lemonade
1 squeeze of lime
1 lime wedge

1 Combine the Grand Marnier, Chambord, lemonade, and lime juice in a cocktail shaker with ice.

2 Cover and shake vigorously.

3 Pour, ice and all, into a **COLLINS GLASS** or a chilled **COCKTAIL GLASS.**

4 Garnish with a lime wedge.

Pete's
Tavern

This rather temperate drink does not have much alcohol, so it is perfect for summer sipping and operating heavy machinery. If you want to raise the potency a touch, add a shot of vodka or gin to the mix. You might also want to go easy on the sugar in your lemonade lest this become cloyingly sweet.

NORTHERN SEX ON THE BEACH

*A*NY MANHATTAN DWELLER WILL TELL YOU there's only one reason to leave the beloved island: to get a better view of it. And Water's
Edge, a floating barge in Queens disguised as a restaurant, offers
just that. With a massive wall of glass facing west, there's nary a table without a
romantic view of the famous skyline. And from May to October you can even
enjoy it al fresco as you don your Docksiders and watch the traffic across the East
River. Transportation is convenient via a free water taxi that heads east from 34th
Street on the hour and back forty-five minutes later. And if you just missed the
boat, so to speak, it's not all bad news. The mahogany bar is a comfortable place
to catch a cocktail courtesy of mixologist Nazeem Miah. His version of Sex on the
Beach eliminates the bad—wedding reception flavor of peach schnapps in favor of
melon-y Midori.

There are a million recipes
for Sex on the Beach, most of
which require vodka, a sweet
liqueur or two, and several juices.
The most popular way to consume
it is via shots, preferably at a
bachelorette party. Rather than
straining it into a cocktail glass as
directed here, you could simply line
up a half-dozen shot glasses and
dole it out.

2 ounces Ketel One

3 ounces Midori Melon

1 ounce Chambord

1 ounce pineapple juice

1 Combine all ingredients in an ice-filled cocktail shaker.

2 Cover and shake vigorously.

3 Strain into a chilled **COCKTAIL GLASS.**

Chapter 6

SECRET INGREDIENTS

BLUES ON TOP

MALI COOLER

MILANO-TORINO

CONVENT IN CHILE

MANDARIN SUNSET

THE SURREY

TOP OF THE VIEW

WAY OF THE DRAGON

TOKYO ICED TEA

LAVENDER MARTINI

JAPAN COCKTAIL

RHUBARB SPARKLER

CIN-CYN

BLUES ON TOP

B.B. KING BLUES CLUB & GRILL

*I*N HIP VENUE–STARVED TIME SQUARE, B.B. King's stands out as having a theme that actually works: an intimate but ample space in which to get up-close and personal with performers ranging well beyond those its bluesy name would have you expect. Consider that in addition to the man himself, the stage has been graced by the likes of Gregg Allman, George Clinton and the P-Funk All-Stars, Erykah Badu, Macy Gray, and even Peter Frampton. How's that for range? The forty-foot bar in the main concert hall—replete with cheesy guitar-shaped beer taps—may look Disney, but the drinks are actually quite Downtown, especially the aptly named Blues on Top, which employs the aqua glow of Hpnotiq, a relatively new concoction containing French vodka, cognac, and natural juices. The result is a cocktail whose appearance befits its neon-lit neighborhood. It's served in the main bar as well as the in-house cantina, Lucille's Bar & Grill.

The Blues on Top recipe calls for floating, a technique bartenders use to keep two different color liquids separate. It takes a little practice to get the hang of it: using the backside of a spoon held near the inside edge of the glass, gently begin straining the liquid over the spoon. It should roll into the glass and float on top of the heavier liquid below.

½ ounce Chambord
2 ounces Hpnotiq Liqueur
½ ounce Malibu Rum
½ ounce Bacardi

1 Pour Chambord into a chilled **COCKTAIL GLASS.**

2 In an ice-filled cocktail shaker, combine the remaining ingredients.

3 Cover and shake vigorously.

4 Slowly strain over a bar spoon into the cocktail glass, so the "blues" float on top of the Chambord.

If you've ever wondered what that bocce ball–shaped bottle topped with a gold crown behind the bar was, it's a dark purple, sweet French liqueur named after a town in France's Loire Valley. Chambord Liqueur Royale is made with black raspberries infused with cognac. Into this mix they add red raspberry, currant, and blackberry extracts, followed by spices including cinnamon, ginger, cloves, and vanilla, along with orange, lemon, and acacia honey. Oui, there's a lot going on in the bottle. If you don't have it on hand, you could use crème de cassis, but there's really no substitute for Chambord.

MALI COOLER

RAPHAEL GUASTAVINO'S BEAUTIFUL TILES here are reminiscent of those overhead at the Grand Central Oyster Bar—he installed those, too—and the soaring ceiling height, three-story window panes, and tall marble columns prove we're definitely above ground, but few people would ever guess this restaurant is actually under the Queensborough Bridge. The signature drink here is The Flirtini, a cocktail created at Guastavino's for *Sex in the City*'s Sarah Jessica Parker, who one night purportedly asked a bartender for "a fun, pink drink." The drink eventually made it onto the show and the rest is HBO history. Flavorwise, it's sort of like a fizzy, raspberry Metropolitan—which is itself a currant-flavored Cosmopolitan. Regardless, I prefer the refreshment of the Mali Cooler for two reasons: gin and Dubonnet. The drink was created by Cheick Camara, a bartender here, who crafted a cocktail that reminded him of his native Mali, a landlocked republic in West Africa.

Guastavino's Mali Cooler calls for Dubonnet, a French wine-based aperitif. It comes in two styles. Dubonnet blanc (white) is a dry version made by steeping herbs and botanicals in a fortified white wine. Dubonnet rouge (or red) is made with similar herbs and botanicals, but also a hint of quinine. Dubonnet rouge is comparatively sweeter and richer than Dubonnet blanc.

2 ounces gin

1 ounce Dubonnet rouge

½ ounce fresh orange juice

¼ ounce grenadine

¼ ounce fresh sour mix

1 kiwi slice

1 Combine the gin, Dubonnet, juice, grenadine, and sour mix in a cocktail shaker with ice.

2 Shake thoroughly and strain into a chilled **COCKTAIL GLASS.**

3 Garnish with the slice of kiwi.

MILANO-TORINO

*T*HE SHOEBOX-SIZE BAR IN THIS DREAMY RESTAURANT features an illuminated glass curtain that slowly shifts between sky-toned colors ranging from dawn to dusk, washing playfully across imbibers' faces and clothes. Diners and drinkers alike seem to be looking up in wonderment: The ceiling in this split-level space possesses an ethereal supergloss white sheen comprised of six coats of buffed car enamel. The effect is stunning, sort of like sitting under a sheet of ice. Tucked into the ground level of the beautiful, landmarked Tudor city building—on quite possibly the quietest street in the city—L'Impero's bar is for calm contemplation or quiet canoodling over a plate of executive chef Scott Conant's homemade pasta and a glass of the house cocktail: the Milano-Torino. Chris Cannon, a partner and omnipresent host, says his friend Mario Buccellati, a Milanese jeweler, created the drink with his uncle, famed jewelry designer Gianmaria Buccellati. The name references the cities from which the two key ingredients hail: Campari from Milano and Punt e Mes from Torino.

Although this cocktail calls for Champagne, which by definition means that the sparkling wine must be from France's Champagne region, you could substitute another bubbly if you don't have the real deal on hand. Thematically, an Italian prosecco or a sparkling Franciacorta would be an appropriate twist; so would a Spanish cava or an American sparkling wine.

2½ ounces Campari
2½ ounces Punt e Mes
½ ounce fresh orange juice
1 ounce Champagne
1 orange wheel

1 Into an ice-filled cocktail shaker pour the Campari, Punt e Mes, and orange juice.

2 Cover and shake thoroughly.

3 Strain into a chilled **COCKTAIL GLASS.**

4 Gently add the Champagne.

5 Garnish with the orange wheel on rim.

When many of us get indigestion or heartburn because we ate something too spicy—or, more likely, ate too fast—we reach for Tums, Rolaids, or Alka-Seltzer. The makers of Tagamet would have you popping pills before every meal to prevent the inevitable. In Europe, however, they have a far more civilized tradition, and one that predates all of the over-the-counter remedies we seem to love so much here: bitters. What exactly are they? The term is a generic one for alcoholic beverages, distilled or infused with plant or root extracts, that were historically made throughout Europe as effective digestifs. Native Americans made them, too, but their popularity only grew when they were used to enhance the flavor of mixed drinks. In fact, by definition a cocktail—at least pre-Prohibition—had to include bitters. Obviously, that's not the case anymore, but I highly recommend that you experiment with them to balance sweetness in drinks. Bitters for cocktails are super-concentrated extractions that come in small bottles and are dispensed by the drop (Angostura and Peychaud's are two of the most popular brands). However, there are also sipping bitters, such as Campari and the Punt e Mes mentioned in the Milano-Torino. These can be drunk straight up (à la Jagermeister, another famous sipping bitter), on the rocks, with soda, or mixed.

L'IMPERO

CONVENT IN CHILE

I'LL NEVER FORGET THE UNVEILING OF TOWN. Tucked somewhat discreetly in the Chambers Hotel, with original drinks by New York's most famous Austrian import, Albert Trummer, more than any other bar, Town heralded the era of the "bar chef." The bar itself is curiously small and has no seats (although you can be served cocktails in the lobby lounge), but you're just passing through anyway. The real show is in the grand, low-lit dining room with undulating beaded curtains where chef-owner Geoffrey Zakarian displays his artful, finely tuned creative American cuisine. But Zakarian isn't confined to the kitchen. The "Convent in Chile" is his original drink creation, allegedly conceived while visiting the same. At first glance, it looks like an awful lot of ingredients, a cocktail recipe red flag for me. But it turns out everything is in balance and all those different citrus notes just sing. Besides, who am I to argue with divine inspiration?

There's a lot of flavored vodka out there—everything from chocolate to hot pepper, mango to rose. When mixing, I stick to the relatively few artisanal producers who use pot stills and combine it with fruit flavor that comes wrapped in a skin, not a warning label. My short list of favorite vodkas: Charbay and Hangar One from California, and Belvedere from Poland.

5 kumquats
½ teaspoon brown sugar
½ ounce fresh lime juice
1½ ounces Charbay Blood Orange Vodka
Splash of grapefruit juice
Splash of cranberry juice

1 In a cocktail shaker, muddle together 3 of the kumquats, sugar, and lime juice.

2 Add the vodka, grapefruit juice, and cranberry juice with ice.

3 Cover and shake thoroughly.

4 Strain into an ice-filled ROCKS GLASS.

5 Garnish with the remaining kumquats on a toothpick.

TOWN.

MANDARIN SUNSET

*T*HE INSPIRATION BEHIND THIS COCKTAIL is the color of Manhattan as the sun sets over the West Side from the spectacular floor-to-ceiling vantage of MObar and the adjoining Lobby Lounge on the thirty-fifth floor of the Mandarin Oriental at Columbus Circle. As a well-scripted waitress in a silk Chinese top explained to me one beautiful evening, this signature cocktail is designed for early evening, "when one is in relaxation mode, and enjoying our exclusive Mandarin view of the sunset." Indeed, the view outside is fine, and inside ain't so shabby either, while you relax in interior designer Tony Chi's saddle leather chairs or striking, carved stone-back seats. Naturally, the summer sunsets are the most beautiful to behold, but there's no telling the temperature in this climate-controlled perch. Still, the sweet-and-tart blood orange juice in this cocktail manages to refresh the palate as if it were 90 degrees out.

2 ounces mandarin-flavored vodka

2 ounces blood orange juice

1 ounce Lillet Blanc

1 ounce lychee juice

1 lychee nut

1 Into an ice-filled cocktail shaker, pour the vodka, orange juice, Lillet, and lychee juice.

2 Cover and shake thoroughly.

3 Strain into a chilled **COCKTAIL GLASS.**

4 Garnish with the lychee nut.

Two unusual ingredients in this cocktail are the lychee juice and the lychee nut, both of which can be found quite easily in an Asian grocery store. In fact, you could kill two proverbial birds with one stone by buying the lychees in a can, already peeled and pitted and ready to use for the garnish, and use the juice in which they sit for the recipe. Technically, it's not lychee juice, but rather a syrup infused with the lychee flavor. But if you're a stickler for following the rules, by all means puree the nuts and pass them through a sieve.

THE SURREY

LOCATED IN THE FABULOUS 1928 BEEKMAN TOWER HOTEL, Top of the Tower is no stranger to foreign dignitaries and diplomats. But its United Nations locale leaves it a bit off the beaten path for many New Yorkers, which is a shame, but a boon to those in the know. If you haven't been there, you're missing a sophisticated dining destination that offers full circle views of the city from a room of true Art Deco glory, not some hokey 1980s imitation. The signature cocktails proudly take their names from other hotels of the Affinia group: The Benjamin, The Eastgate, and The Surrey. But there's nothing stodgy about these drinks. The Surrey combines club kid faves Alizé Wild Passion, Midori, and Absolut. Hang out for a few of these and you'll be feeling more like top of the world.

1½ ounces Alizé Wild Passion

½ ounce Midori Melon

1½ ounces Absolut

1 orange twist

1 In an ice-filled cocktail shaker, combine the Alizé, Midori, and Absolut.

2 Cover and shake thoroughly.

3 Strain into a chilled **COCKTAIL GLASS**.

4 Garnish with the orange twist.

> Alizé Wild Passion is a relatively new entry in the ever-growing crowd of fruit-flavored liqueurs. Its pink color comes from a combination of fruit juices and Cognac with an emphasis on mango and pink grapefruit.

TOP OF THE VIEW

THE VIEW LOUNGE AT MARRIOTT MARQUIS

ALTHOUGH WE OFTEN HATE TO ADMIT IT, and will sometimes go out of our way to avoid it, New Yorkers are genuinely captivated by Times Square. And there are few vantage points as well conceived, and literally as dizzying, as The View Lounge, which rotates 360 degrees on the forty-seventh floor of the Marriott Marquis. The newly renovated View is now as dazzling inside as out. And best of all, cocktails were created by my old pal Dale DeGroff, New York's original proponent of fresh juice and soda in all cocktails. In fact the first thing DeGroff did when he came to the Marriott was rip that bartender's crutch, the soda gun, right out of the wall. For the Top of the View cocktail, DeGroff offers a token from the tiki era, loaded with fresh juice and flavorful rums. It's the perfect sipper as you take a lazy spin around the town.

2 ounces pineapple juice

2 ounces fresh orange juice

2 ounces guava juice

1 ounce fresh lemon juice

1 ounce Myers's Original Dark Rum

1 ounce Malibu Rum Coconut

Splash of grenadine

1 orange wheel

1 In an ice-filled cocktail shaker, combine the juices, rums, and grenadine.

2 Cover and shake thoroughly.

3 Strain into an ice-filled HURRICANE GLASS.

4 Garnish with the orange wheel.

Growing up in suburban New Jersey, my buddies and I would make early forays into the City—specifically to Times Square, which represented the forbidden, dark underbelly of this great town, filled with peep shows, fake ID shops, and litter-strewn streets. But thanks largely to the efforts of Mayor Rudy Giuliani from 1994 to 2002, Times Square is now a hot tourist destination, housing several towering movie theaters and stores from Disney and Warner Brothers. Of course, being New Yorkers, locals will occasionally be heard longing for the dangerous days of yore.

You can find guava juice in cans in the Latin area of many supermarkets; in New York most corner bodegas carry it. The Goya brand is most common. Use leftover juice with seltzer for a delicious spritzer.

WAY OF THE DRAGON

*T*HE OPULENT MARBLE-AND-MIRROR DÉCOR may come from Old New York (actually the Biltmore Hotel, next door to Grand Central Terminal), but the lively flavors are directly from Asia. Executive chef Gary Robins borrows the best from Japan, India, and the Pacific Rim to create fiery yet balanced cuisine. And that deft touch is mimicked in the cocktails, like Way of the Dragon, which sounds like a lost Bruce Lee flick. The drink combines the intense citrus flavors of California's handcrafted Hangar One vodka with the juice of kalamansi limes, a Filipino favorite that offers rather gentle acidity. There is also that perfect balance of sweet and heat, in the form of honey and a lip-tingling dash of cayenne. Once you're suitably breathing fire, pop into the bar's convenient cell phone booth and discreetly beckon a friend. With its sexy style, The Biltmore Room is definitely better in pairs.

2 ounces Hangar One Mandarin Blossom
1 ounce kalamansi lime juice
½ ounce honey
Several fresh mint leaves
½ ounce sour mix
Ground cayenne pepper

1 Combine the vodka, juice, honey, mint, and sour mix in a cocktail shaker with ice.

2 Cover and shake vigorously.

3 Strain into a chilled **COCKTAIL GLASS.**

4 Top with several dashes of cayenne.

Honey is a great cocktail sweetener, popular in Prohibition-era favorites like the Bee's Knees. However, it can be difficult to work with, especially when you're in a hurry. To speed things up, dilute the honey with a little water to thin it and store in a squeeze bottle. It will also blend more easily in the shaker.

TOKYO ICED TEA

*T*HIS TINY BROOKLYN BOÎTE HAS NO KITCHEN, but still manages to put out some wine-friendly food—whether it's spicy Serrano ham, eggplant, or a small cheese plate with quince paste—to pair with their impressive little list, thanks to the miracle of the tin can. And when it comes to cocktails, owner Maio Martinez gets creative, mining fruit syrups in a variety of Latin flavors such as tamarind and sorrel. But ironically, it's the Tokyo Iced Tea that caught my eye. This drink is incredibly simple, with just two main ingredients, one of which is among my favorite flavors of the moment: shochu, a Japanese distilled spirit. Like vodka, shochu can be made from almost anything that grows. But it also bears likeness to Scotch in that it is often flavorful and reflects the terroir of its origin. Sample mixes this exotic spirit with oolong tea, which in addition to tasting great is an antioxidant, or so the health magazines tell me. Now, if only they would save me the trek to Brooklyn and make this stuff available in a can.

Oolong tea has a taste somewhere between that of black tea and green tea. You can find it canned in Asian markets.

2 ounces shochu

2 ounces oolong tea

½ ounce simple syrup

1 maraschino cherry

1 Combine the shochu, tea, and syrup in a cocktail shaker with ice.

2 Cover and shake vigorously.

3 Strain into an ice-filled ROCKS GLASS.

4 Garnish with the cherry.

LAVENDER MARTINI

*T*HIS BLUE-HUED ROOM RESEMBLES A CAPTAIN'S QUARTERS with its deep mahogany bar, swinging chandeliers, and nautical accessories such as globes and a scale-model tall ship. And kicking back in a comfy club chair, with a single-malt Scotch in hand, it's easy to fall into a seafaring state of relaxation. The excellent bar menu also pays heavy tribute to the sea, with daily offerings including fresh oysters and House Smoked Codfish with Arugula, Pea Shoot and Celeriac Salad, and White Truffle Oil. There is even caviar service, a favorite of the afterwork Wall Street crowd that gathers daily. Sampling one of the signature cocktails, the Lavender Martini, I was immediately reminded of the fragrant dish of roasted nectarines with lavender and honey I occasionally make as a summer dessert. Like so many of my favorite drinks, this one first seduces the nose, before moving on to intoxicate the other senses.

2 ounces Ketel One Vodka

Splash of Cointreau

2 ounces lavender nage

½ ounce fresh lime juice

Sprig of fresh mint

1 Combine the vodka, Cointreau, lavender nage, and lime juice with ice in a cocktail shaker.

2 Cover and shake vigorously.

3 Strain into a chilled COCKTAIL GLASS.

4 Garnish with a fresh mint sprig.

This is really a lovely, herbal summertime drink. And obviously, lavender is the key. This flavored syrup will keep well if refrigerated in a sealed bottle.

LAVENDER NAGE

5 lemons

2 limes

½ bottle dry white wine, such as sauvignon blanc

½ pound honey

2½ cups sugar

4½ cups water

2 ounces fresh, unsprayed lavender

Remove the zest with a vegetable peeler from the lemons and limes, and juice the fruit. Trim all the white pith from the zests, and cut the zests into thin strips. Combine the juices, zests, wine, honey, sugar, and water in a large saucepan. Bring to a quick boil, stirring occasionally. Do not let the sugar or honey burn. Remove the saucepan from the heat and add the lavender. Allow to soak for 15 minutes, then strain into sterilized bottles and cap tightly. Yield is approximately 3 quarts.

Cocktail Chronicles

NO LADIES NIGHT

ODAY WE MAY THINK OF A BAR as the perfect place to mix with the opposite sex, but this was not always the case. Historically the bar was the domain of men only (as seen at T. E. Fitzgerald's, 1912, below). In the early twentieth century, respectable women were not expected to be seen in bars; an unescorted woman was assumed to be a prostitute. However, some intrepid women did engage in the practice of "rushing the growler," or buying beer at a saloon to be taken home. During Prohibition, speakeasies, having thrown convention to the wind by operating illegally, allowed relaxed codes of decorum. Flappers, decked out for dancing, drank where they liked, though it was still scandalous to do so unaccompanied. Post-Prohibition, segregation of the sexes reasserted itself. Hotels offered "men's bars" and the ladies on their part had tearooms. In 1964 the National Organization for Women picketted the Oak Room at the Plaza Hotel (see page 32) to insist on equal access for women. It wasn't until 1971 that New York's oldest bar, McSorley's, grudgingly opened its doors to female customers. The sexual revolution of the seventies led to the creation of the "fern bar"—where the décor and the service were designed to attract women looking for a mate. In the nineties, the Sex and the

City gals heralded a new age in cocktail culture. Bars were places for a girls' night out; meeting a man no longer had to be the goal. Today, thankfully, women can feel comfortable all over the city and can kick back their heels at a place like Bayard's, which once housed a men-only club for traders.

JAPAN COCKTAIL

*T*HERE'S SOMETHING IMMEDIATELY CURIOUS about the Boxcar Lounge. When you enter its narrow little space with flickering candle-light you feel like you're on the late night Amtrak to New Orleans. If it were anywhere else, it might seem claustrophobic. But on this laid-back stretch of Avenue B, Boxcar is as comfortable and snug as a gently rocking sleeper com-partment. For years, the bar served no booze, with only a beer-and-wine license. But Boxcar managed to turn this handicap into a novel selling point, coming up with such inventive drinks as Sake Screwdrivers and the fruity Japan Cocktail. Even beer gets in the act, with the Black Cherry: ruby port and stout on the rocks. Now a full liquor bar is available, but on a hot summer night when you're in the mood for something more temperate, you can still find these alternative cocktails. Whether you take the local or the express, by the end of the daily 4:00 to 10:00 Happy Hour, you'll be walking with a subway sway.

When mixing with sake, just as with other ingredients, it's important to choose on the basis of flavor and quality. In the world of premium sake you should look for Junmai, which is made only from water, koji rice, and yeast, or Honjozo, which is similar but has a small amount of distilled alcohol added.

2 ounces chilled sake
2 ounces chilled plum wine
1 maraschino cherry

1 Combine sake and plum wine in an ice-filled cocktail shaker.

2 Cover and shake vigorously.

3 Strain into a chilled COCKTAIL GLASS.

4 Garnish with the maraschino cherry.

RHUBARB SPARKLER

*G*RAMERCY TAVERN HAS A WELL-DESERVED REPUTATION as one of Danny Meyer's, and New York's, finest eateries—a place where the food, rustic décor, and truly professional servers are all of the highest order. And for those who lack the budget or the planning skills to score a coveted dining reservation, the Tavern Room is good choice for a spontaneous drink. With many of the same inspired flavor combinations that grace the main menu, the bar menu is another great way to sample chef Tom Colicchio's cuisine. Many of the Gramercy drinks use ingredients swiped directly from the food menu and are prepared with similar intricacy. In spring you may find rhubarb featured in a salt-baked salmon dish—and also in a sparkling cocktail. The tart rhubarb is amazing with the Caribbean flavors of spiced rum and sweet vanilla, which make me imagine this drink alongside grilled lobster.

1 quart diced rhubarb (about 10 stalks)

1 quart simple syrup

1 knob of ginger, about 1 inch long, peeled and diced

2 tablespoons whole black peppercorns

Zest of 1 lime, in strips

1 vanilla bean, split

¾ ounce Captain Morgan Original Spiced Rum

Prosecco

1 Place the rhubarb in a nonreactive metal mixing bowl.

2 Combine the simple syrup, ginger, peppercorns, lime zest, and vanilla bean in a medium saucepan. Heat the mixture to near boiling.

3 Strain the heated liquid over the rhubarb. Add a few pieces of the ginger and the vanilla bean from the strainer to the rhubarb.

4 Cover the bowl with plastic wrap and swirl to agitate and cook the fruit. Allow the rhubarb mixture to rest for 10 minutes.

5 Transfer the mixture to another nonreactive container with a tight-fitting lid; add the rum, cover, and refrigerate.

6 To prepare the drink: Fill a **CHAMPAGNE FLUTE** with crushed ice.

7 Add 2 tablespoons of the rhubarb mix to the glass, and top with chilled Prosecco.

MAKES 10 DRINKS

This drink may seem complex, but in reality you can do most of the preparation in advance. When it comes time to entertain, you'll be churning these out with Gramercy Tavern efficiency, and enjoying the same accolades.

CIN-CYN

*T*HE FLAVORS AT THIS BEAUTIFULLY-LIT ITALIAN EATERY are about as distinctive as the two magnanimous owners, Mario Batali and Joe Bastianich. The haute Italian specialties include fresh twists on regional favorites; in addition to more traditional stuffings, Mario packs pasta with mint, goose liver, or beef cheeks. My good buddy David Lynch heads the impressive wine and bar program, and I'm not surprised to see him taking some successful liberties with classic recipes. His Cin-Cyn cocktail, pronounced "chin-chin," starts on the road toward a traditional Negroni, but rather than heading straight on to Campari, Lynch detours with the equally bitter Cynar, made from artichokes. As a guy raised sipping Campari-and-OJs as a Sunday *aperitivo*, I find it's a natural kick-off to any meal. The name itself is a play on an Italian toast as well as the drink of half and half sweet and dry vermouth, and the drink is an *aperitivo* in the true Italian tradition, perfect to prepare the diner for molto food.

The Junipero Gin used in this drink makes it distinctly American. Not only does this gin hail from the Maytag Distillery in San Francisco, but the high proof and generous pour make this a drink that would last any true Italian through an entire evening.

2 ounces Junipero Gin
½ ounce Cinzano Sweet Vermouth
½ ounce Cynar
Splash of fresh orange juice
Orange bitters
1 orange twist

1 Combine the gin, vermouth, Cynar, and orange juice in an ice-filled cocktail shaker.

2 Cover and shake vigorously.

3 Strain into a chilled COCKTAIL GLASS.

4 Top the drink with several dashes of orange bitters and garnish with the orange twist.

Chapter 7

HOUSE SPIRITS

STONE ROSE COCKTAIL

COMPASS COCKTAIL

BARBITO

ES SAADA

VERLAINE

STRAT-O-SPHERE

GENE TUNNEY COCKTAIL

BUBBLE MARGARITA

FORMULA 44

MOROCCAN MARGARITA

TAO-TINI

THE PALACE HIGH TEA

STONE ROSE COCKTAIL

STONE ROSE LOUNGE

*T*HE STONE ROSE SEEMS LIKE A COMPLETE DEPARTURE for nightlife mogul Randy Gerber and his Midnight Oil Company, whose other venues include the Whiskey bars located in W hotels around the city and country. All of those w's add up to all-white décors at those other venues, whereas the Stone Rose is (minimally) colorful, but nonetheless sleek and cool in design. Floor-to-ceiling rosewood panels and stone accents give Stone Rose Lounge a gentlemen's club elegance that's completely unexpected. While the look and feel are spare, it lets the stunning view across Columbus Circle and Central Park do all the work. The bartenders here are usually women who comport themselves like supermodels of average human height, and actually make eye contact. They fit the scene perfectly, and make cocktails, I imagine, better than any real supermodel would. The Stone Rose Cocktail takes inspiration from a Manhattan by balancing smoky-sweet Woodford Reserve bourbon with silky-tart Grand Marnier. It's delicious.

Stone Rose Cocktail was created as an homage to Labrot & Graham's Woodford Reserve, a 90-proof beauty of a bourbon made in Versailles, in the heart of Kentucky's horse country. This whiskey is said to have a unique, unmatched flavor that's achieved by blending hand-selected barrels of aged whiskey with the famous limestone water of Kentucky's Bluegrass region. Of course, you could substitute any bourbon, but expect the flavor to be different.

1½ ounces Woodford Reserve
½ ounce Grand Marnier
1 ounce white cranberry juice
Splash of fresh sour mix
Splash of simple syrup
1 maraschino cherry

1 In a cocktail shaker, combine all the ingredients except the cherry.

2 Add ice, cover, and shake vigorously.

3 Strain into a chilled COCKTAIL GLASS.

4 Garnish with the cherry.

COMPASS COCKTAIL

THE UPPER WEST SIDE has been long renowned for its dearth of sensational restaurants, which is precisely why Compass is such a welcome addition to the neighborhood. The plates are global in composition: For example, lemongrass, sour cherries, and spaetzle gratin share a plate with pork tenderloin. So, not surprisingly, even the Caribbean is not off-limits for the eponymous house cocktail. By using Coco Lopez, the same sweetened cream of coconut that adds richness and froth to many a Piña Colada, the drink brings a relaxed taste of the islands to this rather grand space filled with frosted glass and red banquettes. The drink would be a Piña Colada without the piña were it not for the lively splash of Kahlúa and cacao. But then again, Compass would be a Downtown destination restaurant were it not on West 70th Street.

Myers's Rum from Jamaica is a dark variety, which was long the prevalent style produced there. When consulting older cocktail books you may see ingredients listed as "Puerto Rico rum" to indicate the lighter, clear style, and "Jamaica rum" to indicate the dark style. However, you should feel free to experiment or even combine the two, which is often the practice for punches.

1½ ounces Myers's Original Dark Rum
½ ounce crème de cacao
1 teaspoon Coco Lopez
Splash of Kahlúa

1 Combine the rum, liqueur, Coco Lopez, and Kahlúa in a cocktail shaker with ice.

2 Cover and shake vigorously.

3 Strain into a chilled **COCKTAIL GLASS.**

BARBITO

*T*HIS RESTAURANT CHALLENGES OUR EXPECTATIONS of "celebrity chef" joints by serving food that is not outrageously overpriced and that is, more often than not, actually prepared by the chef. Imagine. An alumnus of Chez Panisse in California, Jonathan Waxman continues the agenda of seasonal, largely organic ingredients, and even fires up a wood-burning oven, turning out succulent sea bass and perfectly crisp chicken. The list of about seven cocktails also follows the seasons. When fresh mint arrives from the Long Island farms, it signals the arrival of the Barbito. The fact that the name is a diminutive suffix from Spanish tacked on to the Italian word for beard is cute—but irrelevant. In reality, this drink bridges the ubiquitous Mojito and the nearly forgotten Mint Julep, adding a dose of housemade ginger syrup. It's the perfect refresher for the café crowd spilling out of the raised garage doors onto the sidewalk. As if they weren't too cool already.

Maker's Mark is one of my favorite bourbons for novices because of its exceptional smoothness and mild flavor. After a recent visit to New York, Maker's Mark president Bill Samuels Jr., observed, "I got to tell you one thing. I grew up in the South; I've got my great-great-grandfather's julep cup. Well, I come to New York and see this thing called a Mojito and it looks suspiciously like a Mint Julep to me." I think the Barbito might just meet with Bill's approval.

3 lime wedges

3 fresh mint leaves

1 ounce ginger-infused simple syrup (or ½ teaspoon freshly grated ginger plus 2 scant tablespoons simple syrup)

2 ounces Maker's Mark

Splash of club soda

1 Muddle together the limes, mint, and syrup in a cocktail shaker.

2 Add ice and the bourbon and stir.

3 Pour the cocktail into a **ROCKS GLASS.**

4 Top with the club soda.

ES SAADA

*I*F A MAXIM DOESN'T ALREADY EXIST that goes something like "Underground bars are sexier," I'd like to establish it here and say that few venues in New York are more beguiling or romantic than Chez Es Saada. This smoldering East Villager is a French-Moroccan bistro upstairs, but follow the strewn rose petals down the stairs into the cavernous lair and behold what some have described as a modern-day Rick's Café Américain, à la *Casablanca*, replete with ornate arches into candlelit niches and patrons dining in recline. But if Bogie had beheld the belly dancers who shimmy and shake here several nights a week, he might have thought twice about giving Bergman a second gander. He'd also look hard for a piano and pianist, but find instead a DJ spinning nightly. That doesn't stop couples from smooching on couches as though they're hearing "As Time Goes By." The house cocktail, the Es Saada, explains bartender Salah Abddaim, means "joy," and he created it to capture the mood here. It's sort of a Cosmo that substitutes pomegranate juice for the cranberry juice, giving the drink a welcome less-sweet, earthier twist. I'd love to say that Abddaim created it long before the Cosmopolitan, but I can't. He just made it smarter.

Pomegranate juice may be the "IT" mixer of the moment but I have a feeling that the appeal of this crimson, semisweet nectar will be around for at least as long as cranberry's, especially given its heart-healthy, antioxidant spin. The brand used here is POM Wonderful, which is unquestionably the best, and can be found in the refrigerated case at most markets.

4 ounces orange-flavored vodka
½ ounce Rose's Lime Juice
1½ ounces triple sec
1 ounce pomegranate juice
1½ ounces fresh lime juice

1 Combine the vodka, Rose's, triple sec, and juices in a cocktail shaker with ice.

2 Cover and shake vigorously.

3 Strain into a chilled **COCKTAIL GLASS.**

Cocktail Chronicles

DRINKING ON THE DOWN LOW

THOUGH CHEZ ES SAADA is one of a handful of subterranean bars in New York today, at one time every drinking establishment was underground, figuratively if not literally. The ratification of the Eighteenth Amendment in 1919, beginning Prohibition, meant great changes for the New York bar scene, but not eradication. Speakeasies were abundant; it was estimated that there were 100,000 in New York City alone in 1925. The Roosevelt Hotel even guided guests through an underground tunnel from Grand Central Station to its speakeasy. Liquor importers and bootleggers expanded their illegal trade using bribery and threatening tactics, fostering a major expansion of America's organized-crime syndicate.

Across the city, drinking actually increased during the years of Prohibition, though habits shifted. Beer, difficult to transport because of its necessarily large quantities, became less popular, while more concentrated hard liquor came into fashion. Enforcement agencies were woefully understaffed and corrupt. Thousands of proprietors took the risk of running the establishments, and many became rich. Bribing government officials was a regular practice, but speakeasies were also well equipped for raids. The '21' Club (below), which began as a speakeasy and remains a popular bar today, was fitted with four different alarm buttons that triggered the closing of the bar's five alcohol caches. Other bars were less technologically inclined, such as Chumley's (page 196), a Village speakeasy with an escape route out the back door. When the alarm was sounded, patrons would make for the alternate exit, which opened up onto 86 Bedford Street, coining the term "to eighty-six it."

It became increasingly obvious that Prohibition was failing to curb the incidence of either inebriation or crime, but was instead encouraging graft and corruption. Fiorella LaGuardia, a New York politician, argued that, given its unenforceable nature, Prohibition should be revoked. In 1933, the same year as the repeal of the Eighteenth Amendment with the Twenty-first, LaGuardia was elected mayor.

VERLAINE

*T*HIS LOWER EAST SIDE HAUNT takes its name from the nineteenth-century French poet, Paul Verlaine, who, like many of the patrons here, was ever aspiring to a truly bohemian life, and enjoyed more than the occasional drink. The décor is rather minimalist, which only serves to focus more attention on the worthy crowd and even worthier drinks. Straight from the contemporary capital of cocktails, London, bartender Aaron Graubart includes numerous house-infused vodkas in his flavorful palette—perhaps kissed with lemongrass, or a combination of cooling cucumber and hot pepper, as well as various teas and fresh fruit purees. Of course, he has taken some poetic license in creating a namesake cocktail for Verlaine. The man allegedly drank only absinthe, beer, and rum-and-water. And considering his ill temperament, it would have been risky to offer him anything else—even a drink such as this, with its searing ginger, vibrancy, and freshness that lift the senses.

1 teaspoon finely chopped fresh ginger
1 pinch sugar
1 ounce Asian pear sake, such as Momokawa
1 ounce vodka
2 ounces apple juice
2 lemon twists

1 Combine the ginger and sugar in a cocktail shaker, and muddle until a nice amount of juice has been extracted from the ginger.

2 Add the sake, vodka, apple juice, and ice to the shaker.

3 Cover and shake vigorously.

4 Strain into a chilled COCKTAIL GLASS.

5 Garnish with the lemon twists.

Verlaine's bartenders are adept at mixing drinks with sake, a Japanese rice-based alcohol that is considered either a wine or beer, depending on whom you ask (and whose liquor laws you're following). It's popular for cooking and drinking, and the Saketini has gone beyond a novel creation to become a nationwide phenomenon. To make a Saketini, stir together 2½ ounces of gin or vodka with ¼ ounce of sake in an ice-filled shaker, strain into a cocktail glass, and garnish with an olive.

STRAT-O-SPHERE

STRATA

*I*N NEW YORK, EVEN SUCCESSFUL RESTAURANTS occasionally have to reinvent themselves, and so, after a decade of lavish private parties, the cavernous Art Deco–era space known as Metronome became Strata. The space has always been so impressive that there's little one can do to improve upon it. The addition of hanging cobalt lights from the high ceiling lends a fresh, celestial air. But the major change is in the kitchen, where chef Michael Kaphan, formerly of Zoë, has replaced the Mediterranean fare with haute comfort cuisine, including Mac 'n' Cheese with Black Truffle and Porcini, and Meatloaf the likes of which mama never imagined. The new cocktail list is similarly trendy with such hip flavors as green tea (The Flatiron Green Tea) and pomegranate juice (The Strat-O-Sphere). The tremendous 14,000 square feet makes this a coveted private-affair space, so it's always worth a peek in the window when you're strolling down Broadway. On Friday and Saturday, however, the masses descend on this hip, restaurant-turned-nightclub with room to dance and roam.

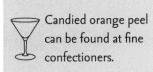 Candied orange peel can be found at fine confectioners.

1½ ounces Ketel One Citroen
½ ounce Chambord
1 ounce pomegranate juice
Twist of candied orange peel

1 Combine the vodka, Chambord, and juice in a cocktail shaker with ice.

2 Cover and shake vigorously.

3 Strain into a chilled **COCKTAIL GLASS** or pour over fresh ice in a **ROCKS GLASS.**

4 Garnish with the candied orange peel.

GENE TUNNEY COCKTAIL

CHUMLEY'S

*I*N THE NOTORIOUSLY LABYRINTHINE WEST VILLAGE, Chumley's has the distinction of being the only bar with two entrances—one on Bedford Street and one accessed through Pamela Court from Barrow Street—both of which prove equally impossible to find. On a recent visit, however, I noticed they had added their first sign: a letter-size piece of paper taped to the door, acknowledging that weekend brunch was being served. Built in 1922, the place is a former speakeasy. And beneath the decades of paraphernalia, including book jackets from the literary clientele—John Steinbeck, Ernest Hemingway, and Jack Kerouac among them—you can still see remnants of the Arts and Crafts design. There are dark oak booths illuminated by slightly battered Mission-style lights. The place offers reasonably priced food and a large selection of draught beers, including some local brews, at prices affordable enough to draw rowdy frat boys and the local firefighters, who have an entire wall dedicated to fallen heroes.

This drink is made as it appears in *The Savoy Cocktail Book* of 1930. It's essentially the dry martini of the day, albeit wet by today's standards, plus orange and lemon. Plymouth Gin was specified then, and thankfully this wonderfully soft and fragrant gin from the disembarking point of the Mayflower is available once again.

1 dash fresh orange juice
1 dash fresh lemon juice
½ ounce dry vermouth
1½ ounces Plymouth Gin

1 Combine all ingredients in a cocktail shaker with ice.

2 Cover and shake vigorously.

3 Strain into a chilled **COCKTAIL GLASS.**

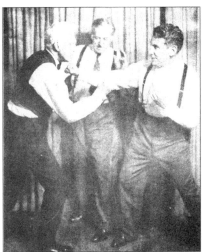

I like that this drink is contemporary to Chumley's, and that Gene Tunney was probably the topic of many heated discussions in the bar's heyday. You see, in 1926 Tunney, a Marine, swiped the heavyweight boxing championship title from Jack Dempsey in a controversial decision. It seems Tunney went down early and the referee took the time to escort Dempsey to his neutral corner. By the time he returned, a good fourteen seconds had elapsed. Therefore when Tunney rose to his feet on the nine count it was in reality a solid twenty-three seconds. Just about as long as it should take to put away this nicely chilled cocktail. The "long count" stood and Tunney went on to win.

BUBBLE MARGARITA

*A*t Bubble Lounge it's all about the fizz—from true Champagne to sparkling wine, there are nearly 300 effervescent options to choose from. And the plush room, always full of red velvet and red lipstick, makes the perfect environment for sipping. All of Champagne's favorite partners are here in abundance, including oysters, caviar, and foie gras—for a price, of course. While the upstairs is a popular rendezvous for groups en route to a big night out, the lower-level Krug Room is the perfect spot to wind down a romantic evening. If you're lucky you'll catch some great jazz, or witness co-owner Eric Benn opening a Champagne bottle by decapitating it with a saber. And if you simply can't indulge in another glass of Champagne, there are always Champagne cocktails, like the Bubble Margarita. The lemon juice in this drink is better suited to mixing with Champagne than lime juice, and nicely bridges the flavors of Mexico and France.

Use a good brut Champagne to make this drink, and it will enhance the acidity without adding sweetness, which is supplied by the Grand Marnier. It's also a very food-friendly drink, great as an aperitif or with spicy foods.

2 ounces Herradura Silver Tequila
1 ounce Grand Marnier
Splash of fresh lemon juice
2 ounces Champagne
1 lemon twist

1 Combine the tequila, Grand Marnier, and lemon juice in an ice-filled cocktail shaker.

2 Cover and shake vigorously.

3 Strain into a chilled COCKTAIL GLASS.

4 Top with Champagne and garnish with the twist of lemon.

FORMULA 44

44 BAR AT THE ROYALTON

THIS SLEEK AND STYLISH SPACE, the brainchild of hotelier Ian Schrager and designer Philippe Starck, was created in 1988 and quickly became "the hotel of the 90s"—a title still deserved today. The Royalton kicked off the hotel-as-theater frenzy, with eclectic, low-lying lobby couches and minimalist design that set the lobby as center stage for models, media moguls, and other movers. They've mostly moved on to Mr. Schrager's fresher establishments, namely the Hudson Hotel, but The Royalton still deserves attention for starting all the hotel hoopla. The good news is it's now possible to actually score one of those cushy couches or a coveted seat at the discrete Round Bar just off the lobby. At "44," the lobby restaurant, you can order the signature cocktail—Formula 44—which may sound like a motor oil additive, but is actually plenty sweet and strong enough to kick the night into overdrive.

If you want to preserve just the pinkish blush of this drink, forget the violet grape juice and go with white. It doesn't affect the overall flavor very much.

3 ounces Stolichnaya Razberi
1½ ounces triple sec
Splash of Chambord
1 ounce Welch's Purple 100% Grape Juice

1 Combine the vodka, triple sec, and Chambord in an ice-filled cocktail shaker.

2 Cover and shake vigorously.

3 Strain into a chilled COCKTAIL GLASS.

4 Top off with the grape juice.

MOROCCAN MARGARITA

LAYLA

THE MOROCCAN MARGARITA, LIKE EVERYTHING AT LAYLA, is only moderately Middle Eastern but totally on target. This Drew Nieporent property doesn't profess to be authentic, and it doesn't require the planning of Nobu. Located on a buzzing Tribeca block with a convenient subway stop, it's a fantastic place to meet a date. Lots of shared plates of mezze—including cumin swordfish kabobs and flatbread with spicy lamb—as well as entertainment in the form of belly dancing further the romantic vibe. For the indecisive, like myself, the Layla Feast is a delectable tasting menu, if not a feast in size. It does offer enough tidbits to get me through the winning cocktails, which include the Layla (pomegranate juice and sparkling wine) and the Metropol (Ketel One vodka with a hint of rose petal water). My favorite, however, is their spin on the margarita.

This drink is tasty as is, but with an all-agave tequila it becomes truly top-shelf. And a scoop of pomegranate seeds will add to its brilliant appearance.

1½ ounces Cuervo Gold
1½ ounces Cointreau
½ ounce fresh lime juice
½ ounce pomegranate juice
Wedge of lime

1 Combine the tequila, Cointreau, and juices in an ice-filled cocktail shaker.

2 Cover and shake vigorously.

3 Strain into a chilled COCKTAIL GLASS.

4 Garnish with the wedge of lime.

TAO-TINI

T ALMOST SEEMS SILLY TO STATE THE GLITTERINGLY OBVIOUS, but it's tough to ignore the 16-foot gilded Buddha that presides over this massive restaurant/club/lounge located in a former classic movie theater. Ironically, the worldly excess the Buddha denounced can be found here in spades. Tao enjoyed their fifteen minutes around the same time that the sake-tini and the green apple Martini struck New York. The bar can still be a tough ticket for a drink on the weekend, but a dinner invitation is guaranteed to get you past the velvet rope. The menu traipses across the East, from China to Japan to Korea to Vietnam to Thailand, with a variety of ribs and satays and tender cuts of Kobe beef (again, as if intended to taunt the Buddha). But the food is secondary; this place exists for one reason. With three levels of theatrical space and the former projection booth turned into a private sky box, Tao is dining as spectator sport.

1 ounce Absolut Mandrin

1 ounce Stolichnaya Razberi

½ ounce Malibu Coconut Rum

½ ounce cranberry juice

½ ounce fresh lime juice

1 Combine the vodkas, rum, and juices in an ice-filled cocktail shaker.

2 Cover and shake vigorously.

3 Strain into a chilled COCKTAIL GLASS.

The current buzz in spirits is all about flavors, especially rums and vodkas, and this drink is a total fruit bowl from some of the best producers. I've always found Malibu to be a little too reminiscent of slathering on suntan lotion, but the new pineapple and mango flavors make a great variation.

THE PALACE HIGH TEA

ISTANA AT THE NEW YORK PALACE HOTEL

WHILE THE PALACE IS BEST KNOWN FOR THE FRENCH DINING of Sirio Maccioni's Le Cirque 2000, when I find myself in the neighborhood without a jacket and tie I opt for a drink at Istana, the less ostentatious lobby restaurant, done up in mellow yellows and polished marble. The "American brasserie"–style Istana offers food heavy on Mediterranean influences, and serves breakfast, lunch, and dinner. With the name Bobby D., their resident bartender may sound as if he's a Long Island B-boy, but his iced teas are a long way from the fraternity fuel we associate with "iced tea" drinks. In my early bartending days I learned that the Long Island Iced Tea was comprised of every clear, bottom-shelf hooch behind the bar, including gin, tequila, rum, and vodka. Thankfully, Bobby takes a more discerning approach, crafting the fruity flavors of raspberry and citrus into a refreshing cooler that's far more Baldwin brothers than Buttafuoco.

For iced tea drinks, I prefer using chilled, freshly brewed tea for the superior flavor and also so that I can control the sweetness. Many brands of instant tea contain mostly sugar.

4 ounces raspberry-flavored iced tea
1½ ounces Absolut Mandrin
1 ounce rum
½ ounce Cointreau
1 ounce fresh orange juice
1 ounce sour mix
Lemon and lime wedges

1 Combine the tea, vodka, rum, Cointreau, juice, and sour mix with ice in a tall **COLLINS GLASS.**

2 Pour the mixture into a cocktail shaker. Cover and shake vigorously for thirty seconds.

3 Return everything to the serving glass and garnish with a skewer of lemon and lime wedges.

Chapter 8

LIQUID DESSERTS

TITANIC COCKTAIL

JACQUES TORRES MARTINI

TO DIE FOR

WHITE RASPBERRY TRUFFLE-TINI

SNICKERS MARTINI

FROST BITE

LADY MACBETH

APPLE CORE

NIKITA

THE 63RD STREET MARTINI

TITANIC COCKTAIL

*F*ORMERLY KNOWN AS CITARELLA, THIS UPSCALE RESTAURANT specializing in seafood is just far enough off Rockefeller Center proper to offer a respite from the throngs. Along with the recent name change, a renovation has expanded the lounge and warmed the place up a bit, but Josephs still pays homage to the sea with decorative "portholes" that showcase seashells. In fact, the owners, the Gurrera family, have four stalls at New York's Fulton Fish Market. Believe me, these guys know fish. And chef Brian Bistrong knows how to cook it, from Black Cod with Miso Glaze and Onion Broth to lounge favorites like Fluke Fingers—sort of a Lady Paul's Fish Stick. The inventive cocktail list, featuring house-infused liquors, flowers, and other exotic ingredients, pays its own nautical tribute with the Titanic Cocktail, a 10-ounce behemoth of a drink complete with a Champagne sorbet iceberg. The drink is a new creation, but given the lavish ingredients and elaborate preparation, I think J. J. Astor himself would have approved.

It helps to have a James Beard–nominated pastry chef like Bill Yosses when it comes to making Champagne-elderflower sorbet. But I've also had good luck substituting storebought lemon or vanilla Italian ice or sorbet.

8 green seedless grapes
3 ounces Cîroc vodka
Splash of verjus (tart, unfermented juice of unripe wine grapes)
1 ounce elderflower cordial
2 tablespoons Champagne-elderflower sorbet (see Tip)
Champagne
1 raspberry

1 In a cocktail shaker, muddle 7 of the green grapes.

2 Add ice, Cîroc vodka, verjus, and elderflower cordial.

3 Cover and shake thoroughly.

4 Spoon the sorbet into a chilled **COCKTAIL GLASS**.

5 Strain the drink into the glass, pouring it over the sorbet.

6 Top with Champagne.

7 Garnish with the raspberry and the remaining green grape.

JACQUES TORRES MARTINI

LE CIRQUE

*Y*OU'LL NEED A JACKET AND TIE (or at least a presentable jacket, a wink, and a nod from general manager Benito Sevarin) to get to the bar here, which is a room absolutely not to be missed. Every time I bring out-of-town friends here, they usually gasp at the magnificently over-the-top décor. For many, the name and reputation of Le Cirque says elegance, panache, and old money, but somehow ringmaster Sirio Maccioni has managed to counter that model with a whimsical side, exploiting the "circus" in cirque by way of an Adam Tihany–designed makeover of the regal Villard Houses when the restaurant moved here in 1997. (Maccioni is now looking to move again.) As one of my friends put it, the best way to describe the space is the Sistine Chapel by way of *The Jetsons*. Since I can't afford to eat here—and the out-of-towners are too cheap to invite me along—I like to come here for an after-dinner drink, one of which is inspired by dessert maestro Jacques Torres. He is famous for morphing chocolate into fantastic structures, but the cocktail named after him is quite straightforward and easy to make.

Producers of good chocolate liqueur include Bols, DeKuyper, and Droste; however at Le Cirque they use Godiva Dark Chocolate Liqueur, which in my opinion is one of the best for real chocolate flavor without overt sweetness.

2 ounces raspberry-flavored vodka

2 ounces dark chocolate liqueur

3 raspberries

1 In an ice-filled cocktail shaker, combine the vodka and liqueur.

2 Cover and shake thoroughly.

3 Strain into a chilled **COCKTAIL GLASS.**

4 Garnish with 3 raspberries on a fruit pick.

TO DIE FOR

JOURNEY'S LOUNGE

*T*HE WESTIN ESSEX HOUSE, ON CENTRAL PARK SOUTH, upped the ante for foodies when famed French chef Alain Ducasse opened here in 2000. But when I occasionally find myself short the $1,000 for dinner for two with Ducasse, I can still set sail for Journeys Lounge. With a 1930s transcontinental travel theme, reminiscent of ocean liner luxury, Journeys is the most casual respite in the hotel, perfect to grab some haute bar food, like $14 chicken wings. And the place is almost always bustling. Here, out-of-town doyennes like to sip a bit on the sweet side: Most "Martinis" are mixed with all manner of matronly liqueurs from Frangelico to amaretto to Chambord. So, should you spy a lady by the fireplace sipping on a tropical concoction with flavors of coconut, melon, pineapple, and chocolate, don't bother asking what they call the creation. She'll merely inform you, "Darling, it's To Die For."

Godiva Chocolatier, which makes the heavenly liqueur used here, owes its name to the legendary Lady Godiva, a Saxon who, according to the tale, rode naked on horseback through town to prove to her husband that the townspeople were respectful and deserved lower taxes. Godiva's three chocolate liqueurs are substantially less brazen, and are instead known for being smooth and decadently rich.

2 ounces pineapple juice
1½ ounces Malibu Rum Coconut
½ ounce Midori Melon
½ ounce Godiva Dark Chocolate Liqueur

1 In an ice-filled cocktail shaker, combine all ingredients.

2 Cover and shake thoroughly.

3 Strain into a chilled **COCKTAIL GLASS**.

Cocktail Chronicles
A PLACE FOR US

*J*UST AS BARS IN NEW YORK WERE SHAPED, but not deterred, by the laws of Prohibition, so did gay bars adapt and finally emerge from a series of restrictive laws. Prohibition blurred the lines of acceptability in New York bars and in the Roaring Twenties a greater tolerance prevailed. But after its repeal, the law came down hard. Only certain kinds of establishments were now respectable. For the gay community of New York, this meant that special attention was being paid to bars frequented by homosexual clientele. In the late 1930s, the State Liquor Authority (SLA) dispatched agents to search out these bars, collecting bribes and sometimes shutting them down. Since some places were closed just for tolerating the presence of openly gay customers, the SLA inadvertently encouraged the creation of exclusively gay bars. Through the 1950s, gay bars were short-lived but plentiful, popping up in Harlem, Greenwich Village, and around Times Square. Like the speakeasies during Prohibition, the gay bars often operated under the control of the Mafia, which organized payments to government officials to keep them safe from raids.

After decades of corruption, the gay bar scene underwent upheaval in June of 1969 when riots broke out during a raid at the Stonewall Inn in Greenwich Village (below). Though SLA had recently overturned the policies that made gay bars illegal, the establishments were still subject to harassment by police. One night when cops ambushed the Stonewall, the clientele refused to disperse and mocked the policemen. Violence broke out, and the city sent in anti-riot officers. Protests were repeated at the site for the next several days. Gay bars came out from the shadows in following decades as the gay civil rights movement gained momentum. Today gay bars abound in the city and, as XL has done in the Meatpacking District, often seed New York neighborhoods with popularity before straight crowds follow.

WHITE RASPBERRY TRUFFLE-TINI

X L

*I*N A CITY WHERE "PLEASE REFRAIN FROM DANCING" signs abound, sometimes you have to follow the bass. And often it leads straight to the heart of Chelsea. At this clubby bar, nightlife impresario John Blair has lured the bicep-conscious Chelsea boys with a luxe, streamlined interior and a dazzling lighting system with more hues than Anna Nicole Smith's mood ring. At least one color will surely flatter you. There are various gay-themed nights but the best all-around party is on Fridays, when the DJ spins the baddest remixes from Beyoncé to the Pet Shop Boys. Large plasma screens bring the artists to life with appropriately sexy videos. And the unisex bathroom—honestly, a ladies' loo would have been a colossal waste of space—boasts a stunning fish-filled aquarium that might just help bring your blood pressure down enough to get you back on the dance floor.

I put this drink in the category of "liquid dessert." It's sure to satisfy the sweet and the sweet-toothed, but most of us can drink just one. It's quite viscous and would work well with the dessert course at your next dinner party, or even in place of dessert. I also like the choice of white chocolate, which allows the pink to shine through.

3 ounces Vox Raspberry
3 ounces Godiva White Chocolate Liqueur
Splash of Chambord

1 Combine the vodka, liqueur, and Chambord in a cocktail shaker with ice.

2 Cover and shake vigorously.

3 Strain into a chilled **COCKTAIL GLASS** or over fresh ice in a **ROCKS GLASS.**

SNICKERS MARTINI

*T*HIS BAR ON HAPPENING SMITH STREET IN BROOKLYN IS BELOW—and shares ownership with—a very good Thai restaurant, Faan. It's a popular locals' haunt, and the atmosphere feels like "big Finnish sauna meets 1970s basement swingers' party." In fact, the last Thursday of each month it comes very close with Steam—a gay-oriented party with some boys living out locker room fantasies in nothing but terrycloth towels. Monday nights are more modest, with an open DJ night that draws some talented amateurs to the turntables. The most popular cocktails seem to belong to that alchemic category of drinks: dessert drinks. You know, as in, "How close can I get to creating an oatmeal cookie in a shot glass?" There's a concoction called the Cranilla, but I prefer the possible copyright infringement of the Snickers Martini. It's a sweet and tasty nightcap, and while I'm not so sure it really tastes like a Snickers, it doesn't really matter. It really satisfies.

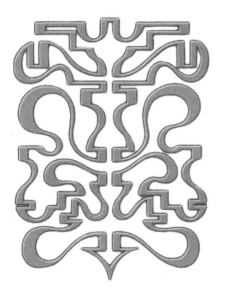

1 ounce vodka

¼ ounce Bailey's Original Irish Cream

½ ounce Frangelico

½ ounce crème de cacao

1 Combine all ingredients in an ice-filled cocktail shaker.

2 Cover and shake vigorously.

3 Strain into a chilled **COCKTAIL GLASS.**

If you like your cocktails creamy like this one, you may also enjoy the White Russian. Pour 2 ounces of vodka, 1 ounce of a coffee liqueur such as Kahlúa, and 1 tablespoon of fresh cream into an ice-filled shaker. Shake and strain into a chilled cocktail glass.

FROST BITE

JEAN GEORGES

))HEN I ATTENDED FORDHAM UNIVERSITY at Lincoln Center, just up the block from Jean Georges, I came up the stairs from the A train every morning, ascending the stairs under the then-Gulf + Western building ready to get my Flock of Seagulls hairdo whipped out of place by the wind created by that hideous, swaying building as it churned the air around Columbus Circle. Now retrofitted and reclad by Costas Kondylis and Philip Johnson as the Trump International Hotel, I hardly recognize the place—nor would it recognize my hair if it had memory! These days, I much prefer to grab a seat at the bar in Jean Georges's adjoining Nougatine room, swing around on my stool, and watch the wind whip the heck out of everyone else outside. In frigid winter I take especially perverse pleasure in ordering the Frost Bite here, made with vodka and one of the best ice wines on the planet, and toasting the next generation of Fordham alums as they ascend the subway stairs, lean into the wind, and head steadfastly toward their futures.

2½ ounces vodka

1½ ounces Inniskillin Cabernet Franc
    Icewine

1 In an ice-filled cocktail shaker, combine the vodka and wine.

2 Cover and shake thoroughly.

3 Strain into a chilled COCKTAIL GLASS.

The vodka of choice for Jean Georges's Frost Bite is Cîroc, a French vodka made from distilled grape juice. Naturally, any vodka could be substituted, but the implied connection is between the grapes in the vodka and the grapes that freeze on the vine to create the magnificent ice wine. And speaking of which: Without ice wine, you can't make a Frost Bite, but while any producer will do in a pinch, the folks at Inniskillin, who make this nectar in Ontario's Niagara Peninsula, have a knack for making just about the best ice wines this side of Germany.

LADY MACBETH

JOE'S PUB

ONE OF THE GREAT THINGS ABOUT BARS IN NEW YORK is they often transform from night to night, or even over the course of a single evening. Take Joe's Pub, named in honor of The Public Theater founder, Joseph Papp. Upon opening at 6:00 pm, the place fills with an attractive crowd of varying ages looking for a place to escape the waning daylight and lounge amid the red and black leather. By 8:00, you either produce a ticket for the nightly show—whether jazz, spoken word, or film—buy one, or get the hell out. And at 11:00, as the show concludes, Joe's really gets into character, ousting the kiddies as a DJ carries the party into the next morning. For hot nights like Friday, you'll have to endure the unwritten rules of the velvet rope and pay a cover to crash this party. Well worth it for exceptional cocktails mixed with a splash of redeeming culture.

In its composition, the Lady Macbeth recalls the classic Champagne cocktail Kir Royale. To make it, slowly pour 5 ounces of Champagne over 1 ounce of crème de cassis in a flute. The drink was named after a French Resistance fighter, Canon Felix Kir, who later became the mayor of Dijon. Crème de cassis has been produced in France since the 1500s, and the black currant–flavored liqueur was first known as a remedy for snakebite and jaundice.

2 ounces ruby port

6 ounces Champagne

1 orange wedge

1 Pour the port into a **CHAMPAGNE FLUTE.**

2 Top with the Champagne.

3 Garnish with the orange wedge.

How to crash a party: As a formerly single guy who has had his ambitions cut short by the infamous velvet rope, I can offer a little advice. To enter a hot club spontaneously, you'll need at least two beautiful girls to each guy in your party. If that's impractical, simply visit the club's website earlier in the day; you can often earn a slot on the guest list with just a phone call or an e-mail.

APPLE CORE

A HANGOUT OF MY WIFE'S AND MINE before we were married, First was our favorite spot to sit and sip Tiny Tinis while feeding each other S'Mores. Ah, life before children. These drinks, however, are by no means diminutive. Rather, they offer several fills of a three-ounce glass from a chilled shaker. With a myriad of flavor offerings, Tiny Tinis do for martinis what the pony bottle does for beer—they ensure that each sip is icy cold. Since my courting days, First has gotten even more progressive with their drinks, mixing with only fresh juices and using the fantastic foams that have infiltrated almost every dining menu in the city. A delicious Apricot Bourbon Sour combines Maker's Mark and apricot foam. And "The Apple Core," said the bartender as he poured my drink into a glass filled with tart, frothy Granny Smith apple foam, "is what happens to apple martinis after they die and go to heaven."

You can make a variety of exotic foams by using a gas charger. For this foam, juice several Granny Smith apples. (If you don't have a juicer, peel, core, and finely grate the apples. Then wrap them in a clean kitchen towel or several layers of cheesecloth and squeeze tightly to extract the juice.) Add some ascorbic acid (vitamin C) to preserve the color. In cold water, soften one gelatin sheet for each cup of juice. Squeeze the gelatin sheets dry and add them to the juice. Heat and stir the mixture just until the gelatin dissolves. After allowing it to cool, follow the directions for your charger. Use the foam well chilled.

1¼ ounces apple vodka
¾ ounce Berentzen Apfelkorn Apple Schnapps
Splash of apple cider
¼ ounce fresh lemon juice
Apple foam

1 Combine the vodka, schnapps, cider, and lemon juice in a cocktail shaker with ice.

2 Cover and shake vigorously.

3 Fill a chilled **COCKTAIL GLASS** with apple foam to one-third.

4 Strain the drink into the center of the foam.

NIKITA

*B*EING A CLASSIC COCKTAIL FAN, I was under the impression that all vodkas were pretty much the same. After all, the goal of this Eastern European spirit is to remain colorless, odorless, and flavorless. Then Pravda taught me the truth. It took only one tasting flight to convince me there was something to this vodka trend. Each flight consists of six vodkas, chosen from the collection of 70, served in an industrial metal box filled with crushed ice. From the slightly anise-scented Ketel One to the light, ethereal, and high-alcohol Vox, I could actually tell the vodkas apart. And once Pravda got busy with their infusions of fig, chili, and even horseradish, this Siberian hooch underwent a flavor revolution. The "back in the USSR" décor would be anachronistic even in modern-day Russia, but the favorite old Russian zakuski, including blinis with smoked salmon and caviar, are still dead-on accompaniments for the vodka perestroika happening here.

2 strawberries

½ ounce fresh lemon juice

½ ounce simple syrup

1 ounce wild strawberry-infused vodka
  (see Tip)

Prosecco

1 Muddle one strawberry with the lemon juice and syrup in a cocktail shaker.

2 Add the wild strawberry–infused vodka and ice.

3 Cover and shake vigorously.

4 Strain into a chilled COCKTAIL GLASS.

5 Top off with prosecco, and garnish with the remaining strawberry.

PRAVDA'S ICED RACK

1. PRAVDA'S BLACK CURRANT
2. JEWEL OF RUSSIA CLASSIC (RUSSIA)
   VIKING FJORD (NORWAY)
          SIGNATURE (RUSSIA)
4.
5. CHOPIN
6. ICEBERG (CANADA)

You can easily make infused vodka at home, choosing whatever flavor you like. Just take a liter bottle of your favorite unflavored vodka, pour it into an airtight container with a handful of your flavoring agent—wild strawberries for this recipe, but you could choose virtually any fruit or spice from coconut to kaffir lime leaves. Seal it up and let it steep for about a week. Test the vodka daily and yank the fruit when you feel it hits the right concentration. My experience shows that, contrary to intuition, dried fruits work far better than fresh. Wild strawberries are smaller and have more flavor than the standard strawberries. Look for them at your local farmer's market.

THE 63RD STREET MARTINI

CLUB MACANUDO

*A*LTHOUGH CLUB MACANUDO ONLY OPENED IN 1996, it's managed to become a classic almost by accident. Sure, we all knew the cigar craze of the mid 1990s would eventually wane, but nobody really expected the city to go totally smoke-free in bars—except at Club Macanudo and a handful of other bars. Here's the catch: General Cigar Holdings, Inc., the largest branded premium cigar manufacturer in the U.S., owns the club, and since it sells its product here, people can smoke here. It's a brilliant coup for smokers—a perfectly decadent, mahogany-paneled place in which to flout a technicality in the law. And what better cocktail with which to light up than the 63rd Street Martini, which should really be called the East 63rd Street Martini, reflecting its opulent address and surroundings. The name may sound pedestrian, but it's also a reference to its price—yes, $63. An amalgam of rare cognac, pear brandy, and Port, it's earthy and mildly sweet, and about as close as I've come to actually drinking a fine cigar. That may not appeal to everyone, but to the occasional cigar puffer it makes perfect sense.

This drink is so outrageously expensive because of the ingredients. Unless you've got one hell of a bar setup at home—which includes a rare aged cognac made from Champagne grapes, a precious pear-flavored cognac liqueur, a 20-year-old Port, and a black raspberry liqueur—you'll spend triple the cost of the cocktail just to get started. An ersatz replica might include V.S. Cognac, pear-flavored liqueur, raspberry-flavored liqueur, and inexpensive port.

½ ounce Chateau Fontpinot XO
½ ounce Belle de Brillet
1 ounce 20-year-old Real Companhia Velha Old Tawny Port
1 ounce Fiji Pear Nectar
1 ounce cranberry juice
2 drops Chambord

1 In an ice-filled cocktail shaker, combine all ingredients.

2 Cover and shake thoroughly.

3 Strain into a chilled **COCKTAIL GLASS.**

Also, I would advise that you think twice about using a color-tinted, squiggly-handled cocktail glass. As the Club menu states, "A drink this decadent is served in an elegantly understated Martini glass."

AFTERWORD: COCKTAIL FOOD

FLORENCE FABRICANT

$\int$ALTY. THERE YOU HAVE, IN A NUTSHELL, THE PREREQUISITE FOR COCKTAIL FOOD. The commonplace bowls of peanuts, potato chips, and pretzels, the dishes of olives and cheese dip that are routinely placed on the bar or served with drinks at small tables are given free, to be freely consumed. But they are not an unconditional gift. They are the loss leaders of the cocktail hour, designed to generate thirst and, inevitably, another round.

Barkeeps have long known that such food encourages drink. In the mid-nineteenth century in New York, many Irish bars served nickel mugs of beer on what was called the Canal Street Plan, with all the briny oysters a customer could eat. But if the beer-swilling failed to keep pace with the oyster-slurping, history has it that the bartender would slip in a bad oyster. And the deadbeat would make a quick exit.

Oysters, which were abundantly available then in the East River and in New York Harbor, sound like a much better deal than peanuts. Fast-forward more than 100 years. Today, some places that promote a happy hour will pass trays of complimentary mini-pizzas, pigs in blankets, spring rolls, cheese puffs, and even breaded shrimp, but oysters with that flute of Champagne or Martini will not be offered free of charge. As for what to drink if you spring for the oysters, Champagne, Martinis with a twist, or that tall glass of liquid cocktail sauce, the Bloody Mary, are the best cocktail-hour choices.

But it is rare to consider the menu and the business of serious pairings when snacking with a drink. Cocktail food is more frequently determined by the style of the venue. So guacamole with Margaritas, sushi with Saketinis, quiche with Kir, bruschetta with Bellinis, tapas with Sangria, and a mess of peel-and-eat crawfish with Juleps make for natural partners to fuel and lubricate the debut of the evening.

At brunch, anything goes with Bloody Marys and Mimosas. Traditionally, brunch is the one meal that is consumed while sipping a cocktail. Can one assume, then, that omelettes, bagels with smoked salmon, waffles, and Cobb salads are fine pairings with spicy tomato juice and vodka, or Champagne with orange juice? Probably not. But it does not matter. In fact, to reverse the Canal Street Plan or the happy hour, many brunch venues give away the drinks just to sell the food.

Now, however, cocktails with small plates have started replacing dinner. An easy explanation of the proliferation of busy bars and designer cocktails in New York is that many people who go out on the town take taxis or subways, not their cars. The lounge culture—early or late—has become a part of the New York scene. And so there are many new food and drink options.

To do justice to serious food like garlicky tapas, expertly crafted sushi, pristine but forcefully seasoned ceviches, satiny cured meats, and aged cheeses, the cocktail's sweetness must be restrained. Sharply flavored marinated and acidic foods need drink partners, no matter how creative, that are made with unaged spirits like vodka, silver tequila, and white rum, and balanced with plenty of citrus. Richer, meatier choices, including baby back ribs and grilled sausages, can handle more robust concoctions, those based on bourbon, whiskey, or dark rum. A cocktail made with a sparkling wine base is ideal for taming the fat in fried foods and patés.

In the broadest sense, consider the dry Martini to be the white wine of cocktails and the perfect Manhattan as the red, and match them with foods accordingly. The major exception is steak, which somehow can be enjoyed with almost any drink, and certainly with a Martini.

At the end of the evening the classic dessert cocktails like Zombies and crème de menthe frappés, or newfangled concoctions, including chocolate Martinis, adults-only milkshakes, and fruit smoothies spiked with vodka, are worth considering. They can be pleasant enough alongside simple choices like ice cream, sorbet, biscotti, a slice of chocolate cake, or even New York cheesecake. Or with no food at all. They are probably best instead of dessert, not with it.

EPILOGUE: COCKTAIL ATMOSPHERE 101

STEPHEN HANSON

AFTER MORE THAN FIFTEEN YEARS of being in the restaurant (and now hotel) business, I believe success is all in the details. My colleagues and I at B. R. Guest have created numerous dining rooms, but no matter what the concept or location, our restaurants combine decor, food, cocktails, music, and hospitality to create the right atmosphere. Planning a party should be no different. One or two details make all the difference between a party that ends on time and one that lasts all night. From one party-thrower to another, here are some tips on how to create the perfect atmosphere for any gathering.

- Music is key. Having a Saturday-night gathering? Pick something with a beat. Sunday-afternoon marathon party? Jazz will be perfect. Make sure your music is right for the moment. Go with your instinct, and remember, your favorites aren't always someone else's. Aim for a mood.

- Throw some fresh thyme or rosemary with just a bit of olive oil in a sauté pan on the stove as the guests arrive. It creates an inviting scent without being obvious.

- Have fun snack foods dotted around the room in bowls of different shapes and sizes—when cock-tailing, people don't always feel comfortable dashing to the buffet table if they're hungry. Salty basics like cheese straws, Parmesan crisps, wasabi peas, and salt-crusted bread sticks with home-made dips always keep people happy and reaching for that next cocktail.

- Need to choose a wine? Develop a relationship with a reputable wine merchant you trust—this isn't helpful just with parties, but with all occasions. Have an open mind. If you tell your wine dealer who your guests will be, what the occasion is, and what you want to spend, you should be popping the cork on an interesting wine that isn't the usual party plonk.

- Learn a few great toasts for a variety of occasions. Always make them laugh.

- Pick a few drinks that are sure to please and serve them in glass pitchers. Fill the pitchers with a fruit or herb garnish—it will look like you spent a lot of time and make the evening more festive when guests don't have to perform their own chemistry tricks at the bar.

- Always use fresh juices. People never expect it and it takes so little effort.

- Pass creative cocktail shots, like strawberry Margaritas, on a tray garnished with fruit. It offers less of a commitment than a whole drink, and it's unexpected.

- Plan your lighting. If you don't have dimmers, stock up on candles. Use only a few lights in strate-gic or necessary areas, and use votives and other candleholders for other spots. It sets a tone, and let's face it—everyone looks better in candlelight.

- Have fun! Guests always look to the host to set the tone. If you're having a good time, the party is sure to be a success.

SOURCES FOR COCKTAIL PRODUCTS & SERVICES

COCKTAIL DATABASES

www.cocktail.com
An amazing database of drink recipes with hyperlinks for each element of the recipe.

http://cocktaildb.com/
An interactive cocktail database where you can search by recipe, ingredient, or even book reference.

NOVELTY ITEMS FOR THE BAR

www.corkscrew.com
Complete source for corkscrews, new and old—some very old.

www.spir-it.com/oakhillpartygoods.htm
A great site from Zoo Piks International for unusual cocktail and party "piks," fancy straws, and custom-printed items.

FRUIT, MIXERS, JUICES, GARNISHES, ETC.

www.sazerac.com
Sazerac Company distributes the Dr. McGillicuddy's line of mint and vanilla schnapps as well as nonalcoholic root beer.

www.feebrothers.com
An excellent source for orange bitters and other hard-to-find ingredients.

www.tradervics.com
From the originator of the Mai Tai cocktail, a wonderful source for mixers and syrups, including orgeat, grenadine, and maraschino.

BAR SUPPLIES FOR YOUR HOME BAR

http://www.bigtray.com
A great site for miscellaneous bar supplies, from soup to nuts.

www.barsupplywarehouse.com
Has great home-bar starter kits.

www.alessi.com
High-style Italian bar tools at their finest.

MISCELLANEOUS — BAR AND COCKTAIL SITES

www.kingcocktail.com
Though not old enough to sport the title "King Cocktail," Dale DeGroff is one of the great granddaddies of contemporary cocktail culture; he knows more than most and shares it all here.

www.drinkboy.com
Robert Hess's impressive site offers a products guide, classic cocktail recipes, tools, games, and articles.

www.cocktails.about.com
Kathy Hamlin's superlative site offers a great newsletter, lively forums, historical articles, recipes, trivia, and more.

www.webtender.com
A regularly updated drinks forum as well as a resource for terms, trends, etc.

MEASURES

VINTAGE

PONY/CORDIAL	1 ounce
POUSSE CAFÉ GLASS	1.5 ounces
COCKTAIL GLASS	2 ounces
GILL	4 ounces
WINE GLASS	4 ounces
SMALL TUMBLER	8 ounces
LARGE TUMBLER	16 ounces

STANDARD BAR (U.S.)

PONY	1 ounce
1 OUNCE	3 centiliters
JIGGER/SHOT	1.5 ounces
MIXING GLASS	16 ounces
SPLASH	½ ounce

OTHER MEASURES

1 dash	⅙ teaspoon
6 drops	1 dash
12 dashes	1 teaspoon
1 teaspoon	⅛ ounce
2 teaspoons	¼ ounce
1 tablespoon	½ ounce
2 tablespoons	1 ounce
¼ cup	2 ounces
½ cup	4 ounces
1 cup or ½ pint	8 ounces
2 cups or 1 pint	16 ounces
4 cups or 1 quart	32 ounces

BOTTLE SIZES

Split = 187 ml = 6.4 ounces

Half bottle = 375 ml = 12.7 ounces

Fifth = 750 ml = 25.4 ounces

Liter = 33.8 ounces

Magnum = 1.5 liters = 2 wine bottles

Jeroboam = 3 liters = 4 wine bottles

SELECTED BIBLIOGRAPHY

Barty-King, Anton and Hugh Massel. Rum, Yesterday and Today. London: Heidelberg Publishing, 1983.

Bergeron, Victor J. Trader Vic's Rum Cookery & Drinkery. New York: Doubleday, 1974.

Brown, John Hull. Early American Beverages. New York: Crown Books, 1966.

Carroll, Andrew Barr. Drink, A Social History of America. New York: Graf Publishing, 1999.

Crockett, Albert Stevens. Old Waldorf Days. Aventine Press, 1931.

Cunningham, Stephen Kittredge. The Bartender's Black Book. USA: (self-published), 1994.

David, Elizabeth. Harvest of the Cold Months: The Social History of Ice and Ices. New York: Viking Press, 1994.

DeGroff, Dale. The Craft of the Cocktail: Everything You Need to Know to Be a Master Bartender. New York: Clarkson Potter, 2002.

Duffy, Patrick Gavin. The Official Mixer's Manual. New York: Blue Ribbon, 1940, Alta Publications, 1934.

Edmunds, Lowell. Martini, Straight Up: The Classic American Cocktail. Baltimore: Johns Hopkins University Press, 1998.

Embury, David A. The Fine Art of Mixing Drinks. New York: Doubleday & Co., 1948.

de Fleury, R. 1800 and All That—Drinks Ancient and Modern. New York: 1937.

Foley, Raymond. The Ultimate Cocktail Book. Foley Publishing, 1999.

Foley, Raymond. Williams-Sonoma Bar Guide. New York: Williams-Sonoma/Time Life, 1999.

Gale, Hyman and Gerald F. Marco. The How and When. Marco Importing Co., 1940.

Gavin, Patrick. The Bartender's Guide. Duffy, 1934.

Goodwin, Betty. Hollywood du Jour. Los Angeles: Angel City Press, 1993.

Grimes, William. Straight Up or On The Rocks. New York: Simon & Schuster, 1993.

Haimo, Oscar. Cocktail & Wine Digest. 1945.

Haas, Irvin. Inns and Taverns. New York: Arco Publishing Co., Inc., 1972.

Hills, Phillip. Appreciating Whisky: The Connoisseur's Guide to Nosing, Tasting and Enjoying Scotch. New York: HarperCollins, 2000.

Jeffs, Julian. Little Dictionary of Drink. London: Pelham Books, 1973.

Kappeler, George J. Modern American Drinks. Saafield Publishing Co., 1900.

Loeb, Robert H., Jr. Nip Ahoy. Chicago: Wilox & Follett Co., 1954.

Mason, Dexter. The Art of Drinking. Ferrar & Rinehart, Inc., 1930.

Meier, Frank. The Artistry of Mixing Drinks. Paris: Fryam Press, 1936.

Mendelsohn, Oscar A. The Dictionary of Drink and Drinking. Hawthorne Books, Inc., 1965.

Pacult, F. Paul. Kindred Spirits. New York: Hyperion, 1997.

Page, David and Barbara Shinn. Recipes from Home. New York: Artisan, 2001.

Paul, Charlie. Recipes of American and Other Iced Drinks. London: Farrow & Jackson Ltd., 1902.

Pokhlebkin, William. A History of Vodka. London: Verso, 1991.

Price, Vandyke. Dictionary of Wine and Spirits. London: Pamela Northwood Books, 1980.

Regan, Gary. The Bartender's Bible: 1001 Mixed Drinks and Everything You Need to Know to Set Up Your Bar. New York: HarperCollins, 1993.

Regan, Gary. The Joy of Mixology: The Consummate Guide to the Bartender's Craft. New York: Clarkson Potter, 2003.

Regan, Gary and Mardee Haidin Regan. New Classic Cocktails. New York: Wiley, 2002.

Spalding, Jill. Spirits, A Toast to the Cocktail. Washington: Blithe Alvin Rosenbaum Projects, Inc., 1998.

Spencer, Edward. The Flowing Bowl. New York: Duffield & Co.

Tartling, W. J. Café Royal Cocktail Book. London: Pall Mall LTD, 1937.

Taussig, Charles. Rum, Romance & Rebellion. London: William Jarrolds Publishers.

Thomas, Jerry. The Bartender's Guide or How To Mix All Kinds of Plain and Fancy Drinks. Dick & Fitzgerald Publishing, 1887.

Visaky, Stephen. Vintage Bar Ware. Schroeder Publishing Co., 1997.

Wenzel, Ty. Behind Bars: The Straight-Up Tales of a Big-City Bartender. New York: St. Martin's Press, 2003.

ACKNOWLEDGMENTS

There's no way to possibly thank all the people who've helped my career along the way, and if I try I run the risk of forgetting, and offending, someone important. Therefore, to everyone who has lent a helping hand along the way, or proffered a drink that inspired me, I thank you—you know who you are. For this book I'd simply like to recognize all the folks who helped make it possible. First and foremost, I'd like to thank my wife, Antonia, and daughter, Sofia Rose, who tolerated the crankiest writer alive while he was trying to get 100-plus bartenders to accept, fill out, sign, and return recipe permission request forms. To my dearest family and friends who also bore witness to the effects of that Herculean task, I owe you all a cocktail. I must thank one of my best friends and fellow barfly, Jeffery Lindenmuth, who lent his witty, insightful prose and keen eye for editing to this book. At NYC & Company, I'd like to raise a glass to Cristyne Nicholas and Natasha Caba for their confidence in me, but most especially I owe the greatest gratitude to Laura Herrera, the tireless engine that kept this book chugging along to its final destination. I'd also like to thank Patricia Fabricant, who not only designed this beautiful book but also lent her formidable nightlife knowledge to this enterprise. At Rizzoli I'd like to thank Charles Miers for keeping his promise to publish me, and my editor, Christopher Steighner, for keeping me focused when my vision was completely fogged—by copy, not by cocktails. For drawing up my very first book contract I thank Sheryl Shade, who acted brilliantly on my behalf. Lastly, many thanks to Phillip Baltz, my friend and unofficial agent, who recommended me to most of the people above.

—Anthony Giglio

Many thank-yous from NYC & Company to the following key individuals for their support and input: Natasha Caba, Laura Herrera, George Lence, Angela-Joy Lifrieri, Lisa Mortman, Sheryl Shade, and Jeffrey Stewart. Here's to the entire NYC & Company staff who tirelessly helps New York City shine every day. A special thank-you to the NYC & Company restaurant committee, who is always enthusiastic and willing to provide insight and support: Stephen Hanson, Rita Jammet, Allen Kurtz, Tony May, Danny Meyer, Tracy Nieporent, and Tim Zagat. Also, thank-you to the Museum of the City of New York for photo and research assistance. Lastly, we extend our appreciation and gratitude to the participating establishments that have made this endeavor possible.

—NYC & Company

INDEX OF ESTABLISHMENTS

INDEX OF ESTABLISHMENTS BY NEIGHBORHOOD

INDEX OF ESTABLISHMENTS BY CATEGORY

INDEX

First published in the United States of America in 2004
by Rizzoli International Publications, Inc.
300 Park Avenue South
New York, NY 10010
www.rizzoliusa.com

© 2004 Anthony Giglio and NYC & Company

PHOTOGRAPHY CREDITS
Steve Freeman: pp. 49, 202–203; Sean Johnson: pp. 48, 76;
Julien Jourdes and Nicolas Goldberg: p. 198; Peter Medilek: pp.
14, 17, 20, 22, 26, 31, 32–33, 36–37, 39, 40, 44, 46, 51, 52–53, 54–55,
59, 60–61, 63, 67, 68–69, 72, 82, 86–87, 88–89, 94, 98, 101,
102–103, 112, 114–115, 117, 118, 121, 130–131, 132, 134–135, 140–141,
143, 154, 156, 158, 162, 164–165, 166–167, 172, 176, 182, 184, 186, 197,
208, 210, 219, 229; Museum of the City of New York, The Byron
Collection and Print Archives: pp. 56, 109, 175; Allison Williams:
pp. 122, 180, 216.

All rights reserved. No part of this publication may be
reproduced, stored in a retrieval system, or transmitted in any
form or by any means electronic, mechanical, photocopying,
recording, or otherwise, without prior consent of the publishers.
2004 2005 2006 2007/ 10 9 8 7 6 5 4 3 2 1

DESIGNED BY PATRICIA FABRICANT

Printed in the United States of America
ISBN: 0-8478-2664-3
Library of Congress Control Number: 2004096490